Life After Prison

Getting Your Life Back on Track

Brandon W. Loshi

© Copyright 2021 - All rights reserved.

The content contained within this book may not be reproduced, duplicated or transmitted without direct written permission from the author or the publisher.

Under no circumstances will any blame or legal responsibility be held against the publisher, or author, for any damages, reparation, or monetary loss due to the information contained within this book, either directly or indirectly.

Legal Notice:

This book is copyright protected. It is only for personal use. You cannot amend, distribute, sell, use, quote or paraphrase any part, or the content within this book, without the consent of the author or publisher.

Disclaimer Notice:

Please note the information contained within this document is for educational and entertainment purposes only. All effort has been executed to present accurate, up to date, reliable, complete information. No warranties of any kind are declared or implied. Readers acknowledge that the author is not engaged in the rendering of legal, financial, medical or professional advice. The content within this book has been derived from various sources. Please consult a licensed professional before attempting any techniques outlined in this book.

By reading this document, the reader agrees that under no circumstances is the author responsible for any losses, direct or indirect, that are incurred as a result of the use of the information contained within this document, including, but not limited to, errors, omissions, or inaccuracies.

Table of Contents

INTRODUCTION 1

PART 1 THE CHANGES INSIDE PRISON 5

CHAPTER 1: FOCUS ON WHO YOU ARE 7

    HOW TO STAY TRUE 8
    STICK TO YOUR GOALS 12
    REMEMBER WHERE YOU CAME FROM 16

CHAPTER 2: USE YOUR TIME TO EDUCATE YOURSELF 21

    TYPES OF EDUCATION 24
        Formal 25
        Self-Development 29

CHAPTER 3: FIND SOMEONE TO TALK TO 35

    THE IMPORTANCE OF MENTAL HEALTH 35
    SHARE YOUR PROBLEMS 41

CHAPTER 4: MAXIMIZE YOUR ACTIVITY 49

    EATING RIGHT 51
        How to Eat Right 52
    EXERCISE AND ITS IMPORTANCE 55

PART 2 THE CHANGES OUTSIDE PRISON 63

CHAPTER 5: PICK YOUR COMMUNITY 65

    THE IMPORTANCE AND BENEFITS OF SUPPORT GROUPS 66
    HOW TO FIND SUPPORT 69
        Housing Services 69
        Legal Services 71
        Employment Services 74
        Support Groups 77
        Counseling Services 79

Drug and Alcohol Programs... *80*
How a Criminal Record Affects Rights of An Ex-Prisoner. *82*
Child Care Assistance... *83*
Mentoring Programs *89*
Domestic Violence Safety Plans.. *90*
Emergency Relief *94*
KEEP HEALTHY RELATIONSHIPS 95

CHAPTER 6: GIVE BACK TO SOCIETY 99

WHAT CAN VOLUNTEERING DO FOR YOU? 99
FINDING THE RIGHT VOLUNTEERING OPPORTUNITY 102
HOW TO GET THE MOST OUT OF BEING A VOLUNTEER 103
HOW TO GIVE BACK 104
Find the Right Mentor *104*
Ways to Give Back to the Society *111*

CHAPTER 7: GET BACK INTO EDUCATION 117

FEDERAL PROGRAMS FOR PEOPLE WITH CRIMINAL BACKGROUND.... 118
WHAT TO DO BEFORE YOU APPLY FOR SCHOOLS............................ 119
FINANCIAL AID AND SCHOLARSHIPS FOR PEOPLE WITH A CRIMINAL
BACKGROUND 122
EDUCATION PROGRAMS AND JOB PLANNING RESOURCES 125
BENEFITS OF EDUCATION FOR PREVIOUSLY INCARCERATED PEOPLE ... 126
TIPS FOR GETTING HIRED.. 128
FREQUENTLY ASKED QUESTIONS 130

CHAPTER 8: SAY GOODBYE TO NEGATIVE INFLUENCES 133

TIPS FOR MAINTAINING THE TRUST AND HAVING A HEALTHY
RELATIONSHIP WITH YOURSELF AND OTHERS IF YOU'VE BEEN IN PRISON
.... 133
TIPS FOR MAINTAINING A HEALTHY RELATIONSHIP IF YOUR LOVED ONE
IS AN INMATE 136
WAYS TO OVERCOME NEGATIVE INFLUENCES 138
REASONS WHY IT'S TIME TO SAY GOODBYE TO NEGATIVITY 142

CHAPTER 9: ADJUST TO NEW ROUTINES 145

THE IMPORTANCE OF A SCHEDULE 146
WAYS TO HELP YOUR PARTNER ADJUST TO AN AFTER-PRISON LIFE .. 153

CONCLUSION **157**
  KEY TAKEAWAYS FROM THE BOOK: 157
REFERENCES **163**

Introduction

"The cruelest prison of them all is the prison of the mind."

Piri Thomas

Prison is not the end of your life; it is only the end of a chapter. Whether you are still serving time or you have just been released and are trying to make it in society, there are plenty of changes for you to tackle in your daily routine. While prison life is structured for the purpose of reformation, having too much freedom can also feel like it is overwhelming when you are finally on the outside. This book is meant to guide you in the right direction to help you establish the real life that you have ahead of you. From the inside, the terms 'freedom' and 'success' can feel so far removed, merely suggestions of what could have been if you had not ended up where you are—many people mistakenly think this way.

In reality, you are never as alone as you think. There are others who feel the same way, probably the people you share living quarters with. You are all individuals who had other lives before you got locked up, and your life doesn't have to end just because you committed a crime. After serving your sentence, you have a second chance to reenter the world as a person who has hopes and dreams. While they might have evolved since you have been in there, they still exist deep down.

Nearly 10,000 ex-prisoners are released each week, and most of them struggle to fit in with the new societal norms. Regardless of how long you have been away, there is a guarantee that plenty has changed since then. Now is the time where you must learn and grow if you want to succeed. Nearly ⅔ of prisoners who are released end up behind bars again because they do not have the proper guidance. You are going to be different. By reading this book, you can be certain that you will survive out there in the world.

As a former inmate, you might live in a disadvantaged community. If your loved ones and close circle of friends have turned their backs on you and you have burned all of your bridges, you need to start over again from the bottom. This is a factor that will work against you, but it does not have to break you. By reading this book, you are going to have the proper resources necessary to survive out there. You will learn how to not only reintegrate yourself back into society; you will also figure out how to better your life from this moment forward.

By reading this book, you are going to learn all about the following tips that will help you thrive:

- How to focus on who you are
- How to educate yourself on the inside
- How to find people to talk to

- Why you should maximize your activity
- How to pick your community
- Why you should give back to society
- How to get back to your education
- How to avoid negative influences
- How to adjust to your new routine

These are among the most basic survival steps when it comes to being released from prison. They will lead you down a better path and show you that you still have a great life ahead of you.

If you ever feel alone, consider that even public figures have spent time in prison. Big names such as Eugene Brown, Robert Downy, Jr., and Tim Allen all did time in prison before they made it big. Brown served for attempted robbery, and during his sentence, he realized just how important chess was to him. He played a lot when he was locked up, and he got help from a mentor he met on the inside. Eventually, Brown went on to become a successful businessman. There was a movie dedicated to his story that was released in 2014.

Downy Jr. infamously got locked up for several drug-related charges. He also attended several different programs at rehabilitation centers in efforts to get clean. Like many people, he was unsuccessful at first. He has been very candid regarding his struggles, and this still did not stop him from becoming a huge blockbuster star.

Similarly, Tim Allen also did time. He is best known for his movies and TV shows, but he was also locked up for drug-related charges in the past. Allen made sure to turn his life around and to follow his dreams of becoming a Hollywood actor.

This book is going to help you. Even if you feel that you have a grasp of what your life will be like on the outside, you must consider that so much has changed. This can feel like a culture shock in many ways, even if you are returning to a community that you know like the back of your hand. The trick is to take it slowly and to feel out each situation before you jump back in. This will prevent you from reaching a point of burnout.

You can use this book to get you prepared for release and for life on the outside. When you are finally immersed back into the real world, you are going to cycle through many feelings and emotions that might surprise you—this is normal! With the help of these strategies, you are going to be able to reach a point of inner peace that will successfully guide you toward the path that you must take now. Allow this book to serve as a crutch that you can lean on when times get tough. You can even use it as a reference to make sure that you are doing everything you can to rebuild the best life for yourself after you get released.

Part 1
The Changes Inside Prison

Chapter 1:
Focus on Who You Are

Prison changes people—this is inevitable. A routine is forced upon you to reform your behavior, and you might end up doing things that you never anticipated you would have to do. No matter what is going on externally, it is important that you remember you are still yourself. Your identity does not have to change while you are on the inside. No matter how smart or skillful you are, prison has a way of erasing these qualities and only focusing on the bad ones. Instead of enjoying the free will that you once had, you are now told when you need to clean, eat, sleep, and even perform recreational activities. Everything in your day is meticulously scheduled, and it is very easy to feel defeated by this. This is meant to make you think about what you have done, but it also becomes an easy way for you to lose touch with your authentic self. There is nothing easy about doing time, and nobody is in there because they enjoy being there.

During your stay in prison, you might feel yourself becoming distant from your loved ones. While you are physically far away from them, potentially unable to see them in person during your time spent behind bars, you also start to feel alienated by society. Life in prison is a lot different from regular life.

While you are in prison, it feels like there is always danger lurking around the corner—this could be a very valid suspicion. When you finally make your way back out into the real world, this paranoia can linger. You might feel very distrustful of those around you, even loved ones that you used to trust with almost anything. Even a kind gesture or a human touch can feel threatening when you are finally on the outside again, so you are going to have to ease your way back. The world is going to be different when you get out; this is inevitable.

The goals that you entered prison with might not remain, but this is okay. This gives you a chance to create brand new goals to strive for. Teach yourself that things are going to be different, but they do not have to be negative. While you are on the inside, your main goal should be to establish a strong sense of who you truly are. No matter what changes around you, think about your core. What do you value and believe in? These passions in life make up the person that you are right now and the person that you will be when you get out of there.

How to Stay True

Your job is not to dwell on what landed you behind bars. You know what you did, and you know why you are in there. Dwelling on this will not boost your morale in any way. Since you have to be there, you need to channel your energy toward something that is more productive. You must remember how to stay true to who you are, and the most important thing right now is to reinforce your great qualities. Promote the behaviors that you see in yourself that make you feel like the old you again. Maybe there are some things that you would like to work on or change—explore these things. Now that you have the time, do some work on yourself.

In prison, you are definitely going to encounter temptations of all sorts. There will be bad influences surrounding you and rigid structures that you will be forced to take part in. This change can be enough to make you forget who you really are. You must try your best to stay true to yourself despite all of this noise around you. Remember why you are in prison right now and how you are going to better yourself starting from this moment forward. If you figure out a way to bypass all of this chatter, then you are going to emerge as an even better version of yourself when you are released.

Remind yourself that you are an amazing person! You might not want to admit that right now, and it could take you some time to really believe this, but you are. You have a lot going for you and such a long journey ahead of you that does not involve being behind bars. Staying true to who you are means embracing *all* of your traits, though, the good and the bad. You might not be a perfect display of a human being, but if you are trying to better yourself, then you need to give yourself credit for that. Learn about what you bring to the table and how this can value you in the real world.

Other people on the inside might not understand you, but you have to stick to your guns. Show them who you are and why you are this way. Teach them about the real you, and try your best not to let prison harden you or change you into the mold that it wants you to fit into. There will always be this pressure present to mold yourself into a common prisoner, but you are able to bypass this situation. When you stay true to yourself, then you can prove to yourself that life on the outside is still something that you have to look forward to—do not lose sight of this.

Counting down the days, months, and years can be tough, but you are tougher. With a strong sense of self, you also have a strong purpose. Some people are going to see you as a threat when you have this much confidence, but this is not necessarily a bad thing. Make sure that you are not doing anything wrong to others, but also make sure that you are not being pushed around. You definitely have to find your place and stand your ground. If you are presented with opportunities that might get you closer to other inmates in ways that could jeopardize your time in prison, you need to be strong enough to decline these opportunities. Focus on getting out and focus on being the most authentic version of yourself possible.

Happiness Matters

You need to be learning while you are in prison, and this does not only involve academic learning. What you have done needs to be corrected in your mind, body, and soul. This is going to bring you back to a place where you can feel true happiness again. Whether you have remorse for your situation and for what happened or if you are still trying to process everything, prison gives you a lot of time to think about what you have done. Think about the person you were during that time and the person who got you into this situation. Are you still the same person? You can change the parts of yourself that are detrimental without losing those amazing aspects of your personality.

Each day that you wake up, you need to prioritize your happiness. This is going to keep you going; it will give you a larger purpose. Instead of simply making your way through the steps of the routine provided to you, knowing what it takes to be happy where you are will help you to bring out the most amazing qualities in yourself. These are your best characteristics, and they deserve to be shown on full display for others to see. This type of attitude can become contagious, and you might find that you will surround yourself with only those who feel the same.

If you can find small moments each day to feel happy, then you have succeeded. You might not think that there is much to be happy about behind the prison walls, but you are still a human being with emotions. There is so much for you to observe and learn. Happiness can be found nearly anywhere if you are willing to look for it. On the days that seem extra hard, remember the moments that you felt happy on the outside. See if you can channel these feelings into your current situation.

Nobody else is responsible for your happiness but you. This is something to think about if you find yourself waking up miserable each day. You get to decide how you feel, and you get to decide how you are going to react to the factors that surround you. While there is a lot that you cannot control, your happiness will always be one of the factors that you can.

Stick to Your Goals

While you are in prison, you should still make it a point to stay true to your goals. There are many different goals that you can still strive for while you are on the inside that will help you while you are preparing for your release. This is a great opportunity for you to reflect on what you truly want and how you are going to accomplish this. Take advantage of this moment and ask yourself these questions while you are working toward your goals:

- What do you want to achieve when you get out?
- Do you want to become an employee or a boss?
- Where do you want to live?

It is important that you ask yourself all these questions because these are the main three practical components of your life on the outside. You need to have an idea of what you want to do, how you want to do it, and where you plan on living. These can all be hypothetical situations at first, but you can start out by brainstorming these first three questions.

Learn Where You Want to Go

Once you see that you have goals in mind, you can arrange them into manageable tasks that you can work toward. Any goal that you have can be broken down into smaller steps. This will ensure that you are still making some sort of progress, even from the inside. There is a lot that you can do for yourself mentally to get to the point where you are ready to start a fresh new life on the outside. Make sure that you are doing as much thinking as possible. Consider that you might need to go over several different ideas and brainstorm before you land on the final one.

You do not need to feel rushed to pick a goal. Instead, take the time that you have to carefully think about exactly what you want to do and why. This is going to give you direction and a newfound purpose in life. Because you have this time to brainstorm, you might as well use it to the best of your ability.

Catching sight of exactly what path you want to take is a good feeling. It will give you a reason to get up each day and to work hard. Being on the inside is a draining experience. It can prohibit you from feeling even the most basic levels of motivation at times. Remember that you still have control over what you want to work toward. Your goals and ambitions for the future are still valid.

Keep Going

Making a little progress feels great, so imagine continuing down this path. You are going to put in plenty of effort to make sure that you can keep going with the momentum that you have found. Teach yourself that taking one step is good, but taking more is better. Try to think about life beyond the next week and the next month—this is really going to keep you motivated. Eventually, you will be able to start thinking in the long-term again. Being in prison can often convince you that you have no future and that there is no use for planning. This is untrue, though, because life after prison does exist.

You will probably need to make several modifications, but go easy on yourself. You need to get used to the new way of living before you start to feel overwhelmed. Take things at a slow pace and remember that making small steps toward your goals is still valid because you are getting closer each time.

Think about those who came before you. This is not the first time that somebody has come back from a setback. You have probably come back from other setbacks in your own life already, so who is to say that you cannot do this again? While this is a big one, it is not impossible to overcome. If you stay dedicated, things will eventually feel easier again. Life is going to have a new meaning, and you will find your place.

Remember Your Dreams

Think about the person you were before prison. This person might not be who you are right now, but you likely had dreams that you were working toward. Maybe you had big goals in mind that have changed since then. Even if this is the case, try to use this comparison as a way to feel more motivated. You can remember the things that you used to strive for in an effort to see if those things still interest you. For the most part, there is usually going to be some relevance.

While you might have to modify your dreams now, you can still build on them like you used to. Maybe you have the same dreams that you had before all of this happened. If that is the case, try to reignite the spark that you once felt. Think about the passions that you had and why you had them. This reminder is often enough to convince you that it is worthwhile to work hard.

Talk with your friends and family about what they see in your future. It might take a little reminder from them to really see what you have going for you. At the end of the day, you are always going to keep a part of who you used to be. You might learn new life lessons and figure out how to navigate the world in a different way, but the core foundations of who you are will affect what you choose to do in life. These are the morals that guide you and the compass that teaches you the difference between what you feel is right and wrong.

Remember Where You Came From

You are a part of a rich history that is filled with other people, the things they did, and what they believed in. This lineage is representative of you in a way that is bigger and separate from all of the things you choose to do in your personal life. Consequently, it helps to get back to your roots when remembering who you truly are. When you are trying to rediscover yourself after prison, it is important that you do not take for granted the places, people, and things that have always been there for you. Whether this means taking a trip to your hometown or visiting people who have been in your life for a while, you can use this as a foundation for you to build from.

It is not always easy to separate who you are from what you have done, but this is a must if you are really ready to start your new life. You need to forgive yourself and give yourself permission to move forward; otherwise, you will not make any progress. With the connections that you still have left, you can continue to grow them. Nurture them and pay close attention to them. Even if you only have one person left after you get out, make sure that you cherish this connection. Taking people for granted is a mistake that most people make at least once in their lifetimes. By making yourself aware of this, you can prevent yourself from hurting someone that has always been there for you.

You are going to have to talk about what happened, but only do this when you are ready. If other people in your life have good intentions and want to discuss this with you, remind yourself that they probably are not coming from a place of judgment. They just want to understand how you feel and why, so you need to enlighten them. You can talk about your experience without having to relieve any of the unpleasant details. Do your best to be patient as you rebuild these gaps in communication that have been set for the last several months or years.

It is natural for humans to drift in and out of communication, but being in prison definitely gets in the way of interpersonal connection opportunities. When you are being kept from society, it becomes nearly impossible to immerse yourself in the outside world unless the people in that world come to you. Give yourself time to realize that this is going to be an adjustment period for you, and it is okay if it lasts for a long time. There is no time limit set for how long it should take you to heal.

If you can sense that you are starting to feel depressed on the inside, remind yourself of these outside connections. Think about how big the world is out there and how it doesn't only revolve around the experience you are having right now. Many can forget because it feels like you are being sucked into a void when you are in prison. Your days are strictly scheduled, and it often feels like nothing will ever change. Know that things *have* to change eventually, though. Your situation is going to get better, and you will have an opportunity to continue with your life.

Your past memories can bring back a lot of joy into your life. When you are feeling down, think about the good times that you have already experienced. Remember what you were doing and how it made you feel. Even though it seems like those times are long gone, realize that you can make new great memories. There is still time for you to feel that happy and that carefree. When in doubt, you can always use your past as a reminder of what you have to look forward to in your future. When you believe that it is possible to get back to a time like this, you will be able to think about your good memories from the past fondly.

It is understandable that you might feel some resentment about your past, but you need to be willing to forgive yourself if you want to move forward in life. Some things are just beyond your circle of control, and it can be hard to accept this fact. Once you are able to do so, letting go is going to feel like you have released a huge weight that has been burdened on your shoulders. Give yourself permission to feel again and make sure that you are allowing yourself to feel everything. Good or bad, you should see what you are capable of feeling.

Be gentle with yourself. It might be second nature to tear yourself down, just as you have felt others do. You no longer need to punish yourself, though, because you are already living with your consequences. Try to focus on healing and getting through this instead of succumbing to the daunting feeling that attempts to emerge. Focusing on the great memories of the things you have done and seen or the people you have spent time with can really bring you out of any rut.

No matter what, you are going to evolve and grow as time goes on. When you get out, you might be a completely different person who is also surrounded by a new support system, but you need to appreciate what you have in front of you. It says a lot about a person when they are willing to stand by you no matter what, and this should never be taken for granted. At this point, it might feel hard to let people in, but you might need to sit with the discomfort for a moment until you are better able to cope with the adjustment. You will see that the person who you were before and the places where you have been will help to make you a better person today.

Chapter 2:
Use Your Time to Educate Yourself

Education is a form of self-improvement, and this is a crucial step to take in life whether you are in prison or not. When you are working toward getting an education, you are using your time productively instead of wasting it. So many people from many different backgrounds struggle to accomplish anything productive because they are holding themselves back. You can educate yourself and become wiser. Not only will you master several different topics, but you will also master some essential life skills that will come in handy on a daily basis. Some of these skills include:

- Time management

- Organization

- Focus and concentration

- Goal-setting

- Confidence

- Motivation

All of these skills are going to become a positive addition to your daily routines. No matter what you are doing, you will benefit from being able to concentrate a little more and being able to have the confidence to keep moving forward.

When you choose to focus on your education, that is going to help you re-enter society. Not only are you trying to integrate yourself back into the world, but you are also working to prove that you can be a functional and valued member of society. A lot of judgment comes when people find out that you have spent time in prison, and it is honestly a stigma that you are going to have to work around as you complete your reintegration. If you can believe that you are a valued member of society, this is going to give you all the necessary confidence to convince those around you of the same.

It is going to challenge you to no end when you try to find a job while having criminal offenses on your record—there is no going back and changing the past. This is why it makes sense to make the most of your time behind bars. When you focus on your education, you will enhance your skills that will make you a more desirable employee. Many workplaces are understanding and offer forgiveness when they see that you have a real desire to improve yourself and to change who you used to be. It is hard to remove stigma, but you are not the first to experience this. Think about those who came before you who have gone through the same thing and continued onward with great careers.

Aside from the fact that employers will take you more seriously, spending your time in prison with a focus on working on yourself will also make you much less likely to commit more crimes in the future. Many people who have spent a long time in prison have a lot of difficulty with all of the changes that come post-release. As a way to cope with these changes, they will often revert back to their old ways. This can include committing more crimes and getting locked up again. You do not want this, though, and you have the ability to prevent this from happening.

Through time, it has become apparent that focusing on something productive for your future will allow you to remain motivated to work on your goals. Having something to look forward to beyond the next day is the key to surviving your sentence. Even when the days seem to drag on forever, you can use this motivation to keep propelling you forward. While you might feel angry at the world for getting into this predicament, this is only a milestone in your life instead of your entire life. You have the ability to educate yourself and to create a better future.

According to a survey taken by an Indiana prison, those who were incarcerated and also enrolled in college classes went on to commit 75% fewer crimes than those without any desire to further their education. Working toward your education not only gives you something to do to pass the time but will also show you that you can make progress, even when in prison. It has probably been a long time since you felt this way about any area of your life. Your education is something that never has to end because there is always so much more to learn, regardless of your circumstances or where you have been.

Now is the time to create a better version of yourself. If you do not recognize the person that committed the crime(s), this is not surprising. There should be a decent amount of separation, since you are working on becoming a better version. You can completely transform who you are with the simple desire to learn and grow. This kind of personal development is going to inevitably lead you to success.

Types of Education

When you think about your education, this does not necessarily mean that you need to enroll in traditional classes while studying core subjects like English, Math, or Science. There are so many paths you can take as an adult trying to further your education. Luckily, one of the resources that your prison likely offers is the opportunity for you to request that you further your education. As you think about your next step, consider what kind of path you are willing to take. By learning about the different types of education you can pursue, you will also get an idea of what you should focus on.

Formal

A formal education is to be provided by every federal prison, according to the Federal Bureau of Prisoners. This law is in place to make sure that everybody gets their fair right to an education, and it is one that you need to consider when you are thinking about furthering your own education. The issue is not going to be whether or not the resources are available to you but, instead, if you are willing to put in the effort. You can completely reinvent your future for the better the moment that you decide you are willing to work hard to get there. Not only is this a great way for you to spend your time, but it will also make time go by faster because you are being productive.

Under your prison's education department, you should be able to find a wide range of courses to take. These courses will range from basic literacy classes to vocational training. Depending on if you have a career path in mind, you should be able to select the courses that you think will benefit you in the future. If you do not have one in mind yet, you can focus on the skills you would like to learn instead. Once you get a feel for what you are interested in and what you are great at, you will be led to a career path that **you are passionate about.**

Some of the most common courses include:

- Literacy

- English as a Second Language
- Parenting
- Physical and Mental Wellness
- Continuing Education
- Recreational Education

These are some of the most fundamental courses for inmates because each one focuses on a different aspect of reintegrating into society. Meanwhile, being involved in a formal education setting is going to show you what you are capable of. Any weaknesses that you discover can be turned into strengths through the curriculum that is presented to you. Even if life seems difficult at first, these courses are meant to show inmates that it will not always feel this way. Life will get easier, and you will learn the essential skills that are needed to have the best life possible moving forward.

Aside from these fundamental essentials, many institutions will also cater to certain vocational needs. This means that you will be able to take specialized courses that might lead you to the equivalent of a trade school education. When you have a topic to focus on, that will outline your career path when you get out. You should be able to determine what jobs you will apply for while simultaneously getting the proper training. This is the most proactive way to serve your sentence and will show you that you can still make something of yourself.

Education gives many people the confidence that they need and the push that they require to see that life is not hopeless. You can still serve your time while keeping an optimistic outlook. There are going to be days when you want to give up, but this is not going to stop happening when you are out of prison. Everybody has bad days, and they have to make the most of the inevitable situations they are in. Teach yourself how to do this and how to keep looking on the bright side of your situation. Education can prove to be your shining beacon of hope.

The Local Labor Market

The training that is available to you in prison is determined by the local needs in the surrounding area. If your area is in need of handymen or technicians, then you can expect these courses to be available to you in prison. It all just depends on what is seen as a valuable skill and a worthwhile trade to be a part of. Your prison is only going to offer courses in subjects that they feel will benefit you once you are on the outside. What they offer is going to give you a basic idea of what is going on in the labor market and how you can work on becoming a part of it again.

You might not get much of a choice in what skills you will be trained in if you do decide to pursue your prison's education system, but it never hurts to learn a new skill or to brush up on skills that you already have. This is going to be beneficial because it will allow you to continue your education in a way that it is also going to be helpful to you once you are released. Consider taking a few different courses to get your bearings and to see what feels right. This is your chance for some self-discovery.

Think about which courses are going to help you reach your current goals. Even if the prison is not offering exactly what you are interested in, there are probably some courses for you to take that will still benefit you somehow. Learning a skill is automatically going to be a productive way to spend your time, even if you do not end up making a career out of it. Think about what each skill will do for you in your life and how you can use it to get ahead in the world.

GED Diplomas and ESL Training

There are two very big essentials when it comes to landing a job—most of the time, you need a high school diploma and the ability to speak English. These are two key skills that not everybody goes into prison with, but you can come out with them. While in prison, many inmates study for and take their GED to earn the equivalent of a high school diploma. This diploma counts for a high school diploma and shows future employers that you are competent in basic high-school-level skills that are necessary for nearly any job that you land.

If you do not have a high school diploma, you do not need to feel ashamed. Many people do not have one for many different reasons. Prisons around the country work to give their inmates a second chance. You will almost always find these programs and inmates who are studying for the exam. While in prison, you will have access to the necessary training that you need before attempting to take the exam. This is a very good resource to use if you are in the position of needing it.

Another common resource is ESL courses. If English is not your first language, you can obtain language classes while in prison. Many of them offer English as a Second Language courses that will help you brush up on your skills. This will help you on the outside by making you a clearer and more competent communicator. Whether or not you have taken ESL classes already, it is always a good idea to brush up on these skills while you have the time and resources available to you. In nearly every aspect of life on the outside, communication is crucial. This applies to the way that you interact with people as well as to any job that you will do.

Self-Development

Gaining an education in self-development skills means that you will be able to use these skills in other areas of your daily life. You can work on yourself as a person in an effort to improve your life as a whole. Whether you are inside of a prison or have just gotten out, you can continue to work on self-development to learn and grow. This is how you will branch out and become a new and improved version of yourself.

Reading

There are many options for you when it comes to reading literature. In prison, you should have access to a library that is full of books on various topics. This is an alternative to getting a formal education because you can go at your own pace while studying the topics that you have the most interest in. A library is going to house books on so many different subjects. This should give you a chance to learn more about yourself by deciding what sounds interesting to you and what you feel you would like to spend your time reading about.

Not everybody is capable of formal learning and sitting in a classroom for extended periods of time. Many people have an aversion to this because of past educational experiences, but this is okay. You can still engage in reading whenever you decide that you have the time and energy to devote to it. Reading does not have to feel like a chore, especially when you can find a topic that truly interests you.

Getting into reading can be difficult at first, but you will be able to really engage in it once you find something that you like. Read as often as possible to fill your free time! This is going to keep your mind working while potentially expanding your knowledge on topics that you already know about or that you have yet to learn about. Reading also makes a great form of escapism. Depending on what you are reading about, you can often get lost in the story or the information being presented, giving you a positive way to get away from what is happening in your real life for a moment.

Reading can become a great habit as both a pastime and an educational tool. Make sure that you are reading for fun as well as reading to learn. This is going to give you many positive effects attached to reading and will encourage you to do it more often. By doing so, you will experience great developmental effects! Your mind naturally becomes quicker to respond when you read more often. This is going to ignite your senses and allow you to explore different ways of thinking.

Even once you are out of prison, reading is a habit that you should keep in your daily routine. This will keep you grounded and focused on something. It can be overwhelming when you are first released because you need to absorb everything that you have been away from. A lot of people find it too overwhelming at times because they are just not used to it. By reading, you retain that familiar form of escapism that you need.

Prisons give you access to libraries because reading is encouraged. It is something productive that you can do with your time while also giving you the chance to self-reflect. You are going to develop your true character and potentially emerge as someone new. Some facilities even allow you to request specific books if you know of any that you would like to read. If you do not have a title in mind, you might be able to ask the prison if they can carry books on a specific topic so that you can get more reading that pertains to your interests.

Another option is to request that your loved ones send you books that you want to read. As you should always remember, you cannot forget where you came from.

Lean on your loved ones to get through this tough time and ask them for some reading recommendations if you are unsure about where to begin. Since they know you well, they will probably be able to come up with many valuable suggestions for you. This will also keep you close to those who care about you and want to help you! Being on the inside can feel helpless, but this connection gives you a way to bond with your loved ones and to keep a part of them with you at all times.

Writing

Writing is another great hobby to pick up while you are in prison. Not only does it pass the time, but it also provides you with an outlet for all of your feelings and emotions. Writing can often be a little restrictive in prison, but you should occasionally be given permission to write. Do not forget to ask about writing if you want to pick it up as a hobby. The staff might not suggest it to you outright, so you need to let them know that it is something you are interested in doing.

When you write, you are practicing many great life skills, such as organization and self-expression. No matter if you decide to write one small journal entry or an entire fictional novel filled with many different characters, this is your chance to go in any direction you choose. Much like reading, writing can also become an excellent form of escapism when you put your mind to it. Focus on jotting down exactly what is on your mind and why. This is a great first step.

If you are unsure about the prison's stance on writing and when you can do it, make sure to ask the guards. They will explain how to do things according to procedure. When the staff can see that you are putting your mind to productive and creative hobbies, this is probably going to fare well with you and how they perceive your behavior when you are on the inside. Staying away from your old ways is essential to not making the same mistakes again. Writing can definitely lead you down a better path.

A lot of inmates decide to write letters to their loved ones to chronicle their journeys. This is a great way to both express yourself and give your writing another purpose. It will also keep your writing safe because you get to mail it to a loved one for safekeeping. Some people are even compelled to publish their writing in a novel after they have gotten out of prison because of the unique perspective they have gained while on the inside. Even if your writing never sees the light of day, it is still a valid and valuable way to learn and grow.

If you enjoy both reading and writing, you can combine the two for even more benefits. Read about something that interests you, then write about it. Even if you do not end up writing an essay or anything that is formal, it is still going to benefit you by combining your critical thinking skills with your unique and creative opinion. Openly discuss what you have read and how you identify with it. If you disagree with it, write that down. Explain why and talk about your current morals or values.

You should be able to get a lot out of writing once you discover what you actually enjoy writing about. A lot of people are under the impression that they dislike writing or are bad at it because they have only written in a formal setting. Writing can be for recreation as a hobby, though; itt can even be something that you feel passionate about because writing gives you a louder voice. You can talk about anything you care about in your own words, and that is very powerful.

Chapter 3:
Find Someone to Talk To

Your mental health matters. No matter what you have done and where you have been in life, you should always make sure that you are able to prioritize your mental health. It often becomes easier just to shut down and ignore these feelings, but you need to find an outlet for them. Many times, it is necessary to actually find someone that you can talk to about your feelings, your life, and whatever is going on in your mind. Think about what you can do to improve your mental health while you are on the inside, because it is not always easy to figure that out. You need to break everything down in a way that is easier to process and to understand if you want to remain mentally stable.

The Importance of Mental Health

Prison can be terrible for your mental health! This is not news, because so many people can relate to this experience. You are thrown into an atmosphere that is completely different from what you are used to, and this is not something that is easy for you to adjust to. The criminal justice system is not exactly known for being fair and understanding. You are expected to act a certain way and to reform your behavior very quickly while also adopting a brand new routine. This is enough to make anyone feel anxious and even outcast. There is also a lot going on around you at all times.

Your privacy is stripped away from you, and this prevents you from feeling like you have any time to perform self-care routines. It is probably the last thing that has been on your mind while you have been on the inside, but it is still a necessity. Again, your mental health matters. No matter who you are, what you have done, or where you have been—you need to make your own mental health a priority. Without it, you are going to crumble under the pressure. Once you are released, you will also have a very hard time adjusting to society again. That is why it is so necessary for you to take care of yourself from this moment onward.

The Prison Environment

When you are incarcerated, you are removed from society as you know it. What you are used to doing and who you are used to seeing no longer exists from inside the thick walls of a prison. You become thrust into a new environment that is not exactly welcoming, and this is probably one of the hardest things to do when you have already been going through a rough time in life. The guards can be very harsh, and the people that you are surrounded by can be even harsher. Think about how your environment has been affecting you lately and learn how to separate yourself from it. This is very necessary if you want to make sure that you are prioritizing your mental health.

It can be very easy to get caught up in the toxic inner workings that exist in prison. It is almost like a new form of politics that you must learn regarding who you need to respect and who you must never, ever disrespect. You are probably going to struggle with these new rules, both formal and informal. Understandably, this might make you want to withdraw from those around you completely. Keeping to yourself can have its advantages, but you also have to remember that it might make you a target in the future. Most people do not like what they do not understand.

Prisons are often very overcrowded, so you might feel like you are lost in a sea of criminals with no value attached to your life. This is a hard thought to face, but it is one that many inmates often feel because they get treated like a number the instant they walk through those doors. Needless to say, you are probably going to encounter violence frequently. Not everybody in prison is going to feel like they have something to lose. Many fights are going to break out around you, and it is up to you to decide who you are going to associate with and who you are going to let drag you down.

You have probably been tempted to get involved with this violence—maybe you have even fought multiple times. This is something that the environment conditions you to believe is normal. At the end of the day, though, it is not productive. You know that resorting to violence is not a good measure to take, especially if you are set to be released soon. Engaging in this kind of behavior can end up adding months or years to your current sentence. This is a waste of time that can definitely be prevented when you make sure to check in on your mental health more often.

When you are in prison, you are being kept away from the outside world. Just being away from your loved ones and off of social media is going to be very challenging for your mental health because it feels like everybody else is living their lives while you have to put a pause on yours. It might never be easy to accept this, but you will get used to it over time. Think about your pending release date and how you can make the most of your time on the inside while still being as productive as possible. You need to take care of yourself to shield yourself from the negative that can come with the prison environment.

Inadequate Mental Health Services

While in prison, you will visit a physician for your medical needs. There is often no option for you to seek help with your mental health, though. This is a huge problem because many inmates agree that they wish they had someone they could talk to. Confiding in people around you might not be ideal because you might have difficulty trusting the other inmates enough to open up. Not everybody is open to the idea of therapy, but this is going to be very beneficial if it is a resource that is offered to you.

Therapy allows you to vent all of your thoughts and feelings without hurting anyone in the process. You can freely express everything to your therapist without the need to confide in someone who might end up telling other people about what you are going through. It can be very hard to find a connection like this, especially if therapy is not a service that is offered to you while you are on the inside.

In many countries, prisons are actually used as an alternative to behavioral hospitals. Many times, people need rehabilitation, and there are just not enough facilities available to house all of these people. As a result, they get thrown in prison instead of being given any help with their mental health. The same can be said for those who are struggling with drug and alcohol abuse. Many law enforcement officers see these problems are ones that are always attached to criminal behaviors. They are much sooner going to push for someone to be arrested than for someone to get checked into a behavioral hospital because mental health is not appropriately treated.

Your Quality of Life

Even if you are incarcerated, you can still maintain your quality of life to the best of your ability. Being in prison does not mean you deserve to live in squalor without your needs being taken care of. Every human being deserves the basic necessities for survival. These include food, water, and shelter. Social interaction is a plus, but this is something that can often be taken away in prison environments because of segregation and various other disciplinary techniques that are implemented as a way to control the general population.

By addressing your mental health issues, you are going to improve the quality of your life. Get help when you can, but make sure that you are still taking precautions on your own to maintain a good quality of life. When you are able to address your mental health, you are also going to have an easier time adapting and becoming a part of the new community that you must get used to. Entering a whole new society where you are going to have to learn the unspoken rules and ideals can be very tough on anybody's mental health.

On another note, taking care of your mental health while you are on the inside is also going to make it more possible for you to adjust to life on the outside once you are released. When you have a way to talk about your problems and struggles, this is going to make it a lot less likely that you will carry them around with you once your release date comes. This is why it is so important to work on your mental health as soon as possible. Each of these steps counts toward making your life on the outside easier to adjust to and a lot better for you.

You might be used to pushing your problems down beneath the surface, but they are always going to rise to the top eventually. You need to be prepared for when this moment comes by not simply suppressing these thoughts and emotions. It can be hard to determine what you deserve and what you think you deserve because of conditioning, but as a human being, you should have the right to express yourself and to work through what you are going through. This is still your life and your own unique experience. If you want your voice to be heard, you should be given this basic human right.

Many inmates feel like they are not deserving of even the most basic human rights because of the mistakes they have made. This remorse can hit very hard and quickly, but you need to remember to be reasonable with yourself. Being able to forgive yourself for all that you have done in the past is a big step that you must work on during your mental health journey as an inmate. Teach yourself that you still deserve compassion and understanding, even if you do not always feel that way.

Share Your Problems

Most people believe that asking for help is a sign of weakness, but this is simply a part of the stigma that is attached to mental health and mental illnesses. Recognizing that you are in need of help is actually a sign of strength because you know that you can be an even better version of yourself. We all need help sometimes, so normalize asking for it. Seek out ways that you can take care of your mental health, even from the inside. You will need to learn all of the rules and routines that exist within the facility. This is not going to happen overnight, so be clear with your superiors when you feel like you need help understanding either. Part of their job is to make sure you are properly integrated.

There are going to be many different resources for you to use if you know where to find them. This is another reason why you should always ask for help if you feel like you need it. There comes a point where you must set aside your pride for the benefit of your mental health. What many do not realize is that prison can actually be the very first place that a lot of inmates feel they can truly change their lives. Because the environment is so structured, you might have several opportunities that you never had before out in the world. You can use this time wisely, gathering wisdom and experience to benefit your mental health by helping you to become a better person.

Once you become familiar with the new environment, it is natural that you are going to meet others who are inside who can relate to some of the same situations that you can. You feel closed off at first, and try to remember that who you associate with is going to take a toll on your mental health. Some people will drain you of your energy until you feel that you have nothing left. Only become close to those who have your best interest at heart. It can be difficult to tell who does, but you will only find out by mingling. Social interactions will become scarce otherwise because you can only talk to those on the inside on a regular basis.

Opening up to other inmates can be healing in many ways. You will realize that what you are feeling does not make you an outcast. There are likely several other people who feel the way that you do. Even if you cannot relate in the exact same way, you are still having a shared experience with your fellow inmates. When you go through a routine with the same people each day, this can create close bonds because only they know exactly what it is like to be on the inside at this time and in this place.

Stress and Anxiety

Being in prison means that you are always going to be surrounded by a lot of commotion. This can cause stress and anxiety in most cases. You are going to have to get used to all of the noise and the constant invasion of privacy while you are on the inside. By making sure that you have someone to talk to, you will be able to better express yourself instead of keeping everything inside. This can be somebody that you speak with about your mental health, a loved one that you have contact with or a fellow inmate.

It is not easy to talk about your personal thoughts with someone that you do not know well, but it helps to try to gradually open up to the idea of talking about them. Give yourself a chance to gather all of your thoughts before you open up to others. This can be done through reading or writing. If you work on expressing yourself in this way, the topics will be on your mind. You should be able to see how these thoughts come to the surface and where they stem from. While you are in prison, you are going to have a lot of time to reflect on these thoughts—use it to your advantage.

While opening up might initially bring forth some bad feelings, you can still navigate your way through them if you are willing to explore them. Address them head-on, asking yourself why they make you feel this way. Many situations are no longer in your control and might have never been in your control. This is something you have to learn to accept, or else it will bring you a lot of stress and anxiety. Sitting in discomfort is never a desirable feeling, but it might be necessary when you are trying to get to the root of what is bothering you.

Once you feel like you might be ready to open up to someone, you can reach out to the health care team, the chaplain, or the wing staff. Each of them should be able to guide you in the right direction. This is going to be the start of your mental health journey, and it is not something that you ever need to feel ashamed about. Needing help in this area is human nature, and you deserve to be heard no matter what. Keep telling yourself this until you believe it.

It is the obligation of the facility to make sure that you are treated humanely and safely. This should always include the topic of mental health and the needs that come along with it. If you express that you need to talk to someone, then you should be given an opportunity to do so. It can be hard to get to this point on your own, but if you can, it will really do a lot for the rest of the time that you have left on the inside. Once you start talking to someone and really opening up about the way you feel, you will start to be a little bit lighter on the inside. What used to bother you will now start to become less important as you focus on your life ahead.

Outreach Options

Do not forget about the people on the outside who love and care about you. If you have even one connection to the outside world, this can help your mental health tremendously. Even if you do not feel like opening up about your own experience, make it a point to let the other person talk about what is going on in their life and what is happening around them. This is going to feel grounding and serve as a reminder that you still have the outside world to look forward to upon your release. No matter what happens while you are in prison, the outside world is not going to stop existing. This can feel like both a blessing and a curse.

If you do end up talking about yourself and your new temporary life, make sure that you keep your loved one in the loop. It helps to know that someone else cares about you and about how you are doing. In a way, it almost makes it easier for you to carry out your remaining time on the inside when you know that you can have a listening ear on the other end of the phone who wants to know about what is going on. It can be easy to lose yourself in the chaos that surrounds you. This might cause you to feel small and to keep quiet, but you can open up when you talk to someone you love, care about, and miss very much.

Once you start to vocalize the things that are bothering you, this is going to help you release them back out into the world. You do not need to hold onto these things once you have worked through them. Give yourself permission to forgive, to move forward, and to let go.

This is a part of the process that you are going to have to learn as you spend more time alone with your thoughts on the inside. Some days are going to feel incredibly long and weighed down if you have these lingering thoughts that are burdening you, but you do not have to live this way any longer. Teach yourself that letting go is going to be what is best for you.

Ask the prison staff if they have any 'listeners' available. Some prisons have a program in place that trains other prisoners to be available to listen to the problems of others. This is similar to therapy in some ways, but it should also be a situation that is far more relatable because you still share the commonality that you are both in there together and going through the same daily experiences. This is a confidential service that many inmates do not know about because they do not know that something like this even exists. It is worth a shot to ask about it because you never know if your prison might already have a program like this in place. If not, this might spark an interest in developing one.

No matter how you get the support you need, make sure you remind yourself that you are just as deserving of it as anyone else. You need to be heard, and you deserve the recognition. At the very least, you should feel like you have at least one outlet that you can count on to make sure that you are able to get all of your feelings off your chest. This is going to make all the difference in the world.

Be gentle with yourself even though it can be so easy to just put yourself down as others have in the past. You might have done things in your life that you are not proud of and that you would rather not revisit, but the experience you are having right now is still valid. You are still a human being who deserves recognition.

Chapter 4:
Maximize Your Activity

Getting your body moving is going to make you feel better. It is something that you can do daily in your free time, and it will benefit you both physically and mentally. Through physical exercise, you can actually lower your risk of developing anxiety or depression. When you exercise, endorphins are released and will make you feel noticeably happier. This chemical reaction in your brain is essential, especially when you are going through something that you cannot control. Even if the environment around you is chaotic, you can still find peace by way of physical activity. Engage in as much of it as you can!

Another factor you must consider is what you are putting into your body. If you are loading up on carbs and sugar, you are going to feel sluggish throughout the day. These foods might be what bring you instant gratification and comfort, but their long-term effects are not going to work out in your favor. What you put into your body fuels you, and this is something you must consider when you are planning out your meals. Think about them ahead of time to prevent yourself from binge eating out of stress or anxiety.

With these tips and methods, you are going to discover that you can make yourself healthy from the inside out. When your body feels better, your mind is destined to follow suit. Think about how great it will be when you have this peace of mind and how much easier your daily life will become. Eliminating stress is a great starting point, and that is exactly what you will do when you place a priority on maximizing your physical activity and eating a more nourishing diet.

Some feel overwhelmed by the idea of changing up their lifestyle even more than it has been changed. Think about it this way, though—you do not have to start a strict diet or join a sports team. Even small changes that eventually lead to bigger ones will help you to feel better. You can take walks or lift weights a few times a week. Each of these activities is usually possible both inside and outside of prison, which makes it easy to keep up with the routine.

Any activity that allows you to move is going to greatly benefit you. It might feel like the last thing you want to do right now, but try to get yourself motivated. Once you feel that first rush of endorphins, you will have all of the motivation you need to keep pushing forward. Think about your active style as a way to feel better instead of to look better. This will take away any of the pressures that usually come with a lifestyle change and will allow you to focus on the main goals of being happy and taking care of yourself.

Eating Right

What you are used to eating in prison will most likely not remain the same when you are on the outside. After you get out of prison, it is not uncommon to want to completely change your diet. You will be tired of eating the same few things, and this might lead to an aversion to certain foods. This is your opportunity to change up your diet and to think about what you really want to eat. The options will be endless, and you might even find some positivity in cooking your own meals and enjoying the food that you prepare for yourself. The food that you have been eating behind bars has been less than deluxe, so treat yourself to something of better quality. You deserve to nourish your body by eating wholesome and delicious food.

The standards are not very high in prison, but you have to remember that there are people working hard to prepare every meal that you eat. Even though you are experiencing a rotating menu that likely features spaghetti, mashed potatoes, sandwiches, and other similar foods, you still have to realize that others are working long hours to make sure that you have this food. If you are in prison and do not have much to spend on commissary, you will need to make due with what you have right now. This will give you something to look forward to when you are on the outside.

Many inmates look forward to eating something different and adding more variety into their diets. You are probably missing your favorite restaurants and home-cooked meals. You likely even miss cooking food yourself. There will be many opportunities to diversify your diet when you get out. This is something that you can use as a major motivational factor. Since you have been so used to eating what the prison provides, you probably have not been getting enough of each food group. Prisons need to feed a lot of people at a cheap price, so this means they will load you up with carbs and fattening foods that will keep you full. Getting out will mean getting the time to change this.

How to Eat Right

Living on the menu that the prison provides is not ideal because you will need to supplement. Make sure that you are aware of the food pyramid and make sure that you are getting enough fruits and veggies in your diet. Your body is used to eating foods that are carb-heavy and fattening, but you can change what it craves by making sure you supplement whenever possible. Take advantage of meals that offer fruits and veggies. Ask for extra portions to make sure that you are getting enough whole ingredients in your meals.

Unfortunately, most prison menus are only designed to give you the bare minimum of the nutrition that you actually require. The meals are not going to be full of nutrients and minerals, and it can often be difficult to remember this if you are responsible for supplementing on your own. Most doctors and nutritionists agree that a prison diet is not the best one, but it can be made better if you bring awareness to any imbalances that you notice.

Getting into the habit of relying on commissary too much can be detrimental for many reasons. You are spending money to purchase junk food, and you are giving up the chance to eat hot food because you are relying on a snacking habit. Even if you feel that the menu is repetitive, it is better to eat at least two hot meals a day rather than substituting with artificial flavors and preservatives found in commissary food.

What you will actually find if you know to look for them in the commissary are vitamins. You should definitely start taking a daily multivitamin if you have an opportunity because this is going to help you with supplementing your nutrition. Even if you are not eating a very balanced diet, getting help from a supplement is still better than nothing. Once you are on the outside, you can keep up with this habit. It might even be beneficial to see a doctor to make sure you do not need any extra supplements.

No matter how careful you are to supplement, you still need to double-check that you are getting enough nutrients in. A multivitamin might not suffice if you are still low on other vitamins and minerals. This is why speaking with a professional will get you on the right path. Your doctor will be able to assess you and make some suggestions for what you need to include in your diet, both food and supplement-wise. Bringing awareness to this is going to get the ball rolling. From here, you will be able to figure out what you can do to make your diet even better.

Remember to always drink plenty of water. It can be tempting to opt for juice or soda while you are in prison, but this is going to just dehydrate you or make you feel an eventual sugar crash. Your body is mostly made up of water, and it needs water to survive. Make sure that you are quenching your thirst with plenty of it, especially on days that are really hot or when you are doing strenuous activities such as working out. This is going to make you feel better both physically and mentally.

Drinking enough water allows your bodily systems to function correctly. When you do, everything will be circulating in the healthiest way possible. You need water to function at your very best. If you do not like the taste, like many people, you can add some lemon juice or other natural flavoring to it to encourage yourself to drink it more often. Stay away from any artificial additives that are going to drag you down, though.

This is a great habit to have, because it means that you are always going to be taking care of your body in a sense. Drinking plenty of water is one of the easiest changes that you can make in your life, as long as you remember to be consistent with it. Having water around you that is easy to access will promote you to drink it more often. If it is within eyesight, your brain will realize that it actually does need that water and will even start to crave more of it. These are just a few steps that will take you in the right direction. They are going to promote better habits that will benefit your health for the rest of your life.

You should start to take your health seriously because it is important. Even with a long sentence ahead of you, you still need to take care of yourself. Work on self-care and being able to place value on yourself as a person. This can be difficult to remember in prison, but you deserve it.

If you are tired of feeling terrible or down, you need to work from the inside out. Making sure that you are doing everything in your control to improve your life is going to make a difference elsewhere. You cannot always pick what you are going to eat or when you are going to eat, but you can make smart decisions like staying hydrated and substituting vegetables for other, fattening foods when you feel that you could use a pick-me-up.

Exercise and Its Importance

It can be tempting to waste your days away in prison when you have so much free time to just lay around. This, though, is how depression can quickly set in. If you do not take action, your body gets used to being in this physical and mental slump. Soon, you will hardly even have the motivation to get up and do your routine tasks each day. You need to prevent yourself from falling into this trap and from getting caught up in laziness. It will only bring you down and make time feel like it is going by even slower than usual.

Once you are released, your habits are going to follow you because you have been doing them daily. They are not magically going to disappear just because the setting changes. Even though having your freedom back will feel really exciting at first, you might find it hard to keep up with the pace of regular life again if you are stuck in a rut of laziness. Think about how you are spending your time and if it is being spent productively. You can make changes right now to improve your days, and it does not matter if you have days left in your sentence or years.

Make this change for yourself because you want to feel as positive as possible. Do not go into this decision-making process with the idea that it is going to suck or that it will not be worth your time. With that kind of attitude, you will probably not benefit as much. You need to get into the right mindset that will allow you to transform your habits. Think about what you can do to get up and move so that you can get back to feeling active again.

It is a necessity for your body to move. If you keep it stagnant for too long, you might not feel the effects right away, but they will eventually catch up to you. When you commit to exercising, your body has no choice but to activate. All of your bodily functions are going to be charged and ready to work hard for you. This is also a great way to burn off steam, which can lead to less stress and anxiety. Overall, it is also an excellent way for you to pass the time. There are no downsides when it comes to exercising, and you will start to see this when you are able to keep up with a regular physical fitness routine.

Teach yourself that it is good to challenge your body. When you make it a point to exercise, you are encouraging yourself to work actively and much harder than you would if you were just remaining in a restful state. You do not have to create a whole workout routine that becomes repetitive and boring, though. Instead, think of ways that are engaging and interesting to get out and about. Even just walking or running can be a nice beginning for you if you are looking to break free from your laziness. This can be done in nearly every setting.

How to Get Active

The goal is for you to figure out what you can do that will motivate you to get up and be active. Not all exercise is enjoyable, but you can find the right exercise that will actually feel fun and beneficial to you. Think about what you can do that is physically active and also enjoyable. If you do not care to play basketball or to lift weights, then you can think about other ways to get active that will still give you the same benefits. There are endless options if you are willing to dig deeper. Think about what you actually enjoy doing.

There are three main exercises that you can incorporate into your routine while you are in prison. They are all very simple on the surface, but they will help you by making sure that you keep your body active and moving. Consider using them when you do not know what else to do. These three exercises will give you a foundation for what you should do and how you should build upon them in the future. Even outside of prison, they are all great exercises that can definitely be included in any workout routine.

Stretching

Stretching is a great exercise to incorporate in your daily life because you can do it virtually anywhere. Even if you are in your cell, you can still stretch out while standing, seated, or lying down. Stretching makes your body feel good, and you will feel great when you do it. Many people do not see this as a form of exercise, but it gets your body feeling limber and great. Stretch and bend all of your limbs in the morning until you feel like you have completely reacclimated to being awake. Doing this before you even get out of bed will ensure that you have a productive start to the day.

You can stretch at any other point in time that you feel like your body needs it. When playing sports or doing more strenuous exercise, it is important that you keep up with this by stretching to prevent yourself from injuring your muscles. Stretching before bed is another great thing to do. This can often make you feel more relaxed and comfortable before you lie down to sleep.

As you stretch, think about how you are letting go of any worries and stressors that you have. Imagine them leaving your body, only leaving behind feelings of positivity. Sometimes, taking a breather to stretch yourself out can help you to manage your anger or other negative feelings that might arise during the day.

Aerobics

This is a great form of exercise for when you want to blow off some steam. Aerobics is basically anything that gets your heart pumping, which is very beneficial. While you do not want to strain your heart, you do need to make sure that you are pushing yourself a little bit. This is going to build up your endurance and release endorphins that will make you feel great. A great aerobic activity is jogging. If you get time outside, use this wisely. Jog around the perimeter to get some cardio into your routine. You can also walk at a brisk pace if you do not enjoy running.

Make sure that you pick an aerobic activity to do for at least 20 minutes a couple times a week. This is going to be just enough to get your heart rate up and to remind your body that it feels good to move. You might not want to get active; it might even feel like the last thing that you want to do. The thing about aerobic exercise is that you can push yourself to keep going with it, and then it will suddenly feel less difficult. Once you get past the point of wanting to give up, this is usually when you start to feel the release.

Resistance

Resistance training is another great way to get some physical activity in. You can lift weights or use resistance bands to give yourself a challenge. This helps you in a different way because you need to focus on using specific areas of your body. If you do not have equipment to use or if you do not feel like going for a full-blown lifting session, you can just do push-ups and sit-ups to use the resistance of your own bodyweight. This is going to give you a great workout while also challenging you to try harder.

Once you are out of prison, you can continue with this same kind of resistance training. In fact, the great thing about all three of these types of exercises is that they are going to benefit you in the same way outside of prison as they did inside. Just like anything else, if you keep up with the habit, you are going to get physically and mentally stronger from doing resistance training. Make sure that you use this to your advantage, slowly challenging yourself more and more.

When you combine eating well with exercising, you are giving yourself a better chance of feeling well mentally and physically. These actions can make all the difference, even if you do not think they will change much. When you incorporate this kind of balance into your life, you will realize that this is a pattern that is actually going to be good for you. It can be modified to suit your lifestyle as the latter changes and transforms, but you do not need to completely scrap the strategies when you get out of prison, which is nice because that will serve as a form of consistency.

When thinking about habits, you can think about the bad ones that you have picked up along the years. Bad habits are the reason why you ended up in prison, and this is all up to you to change. You have to be willing to figure out a different pattern and a different way of living before you can say that you have truly changed. This is going to help you stay out of prison in the future and prevent you from leaning on your old habits.

You need to actively think about how you will beat your old bad habits and why you want to. When you have a reason, this is going to make a huge difference in your life and actually allow you to feel motivated to change your life for the better. This purpose will become your driving force, and it will keep you on track even when you feel like reverting back to your old ways.

Part 2
The Changes Outside Prison

Chapter 5:
Pick Your Community

By focusing on your time outside of prison now, you are going to learn how to build up the community that surrounds you. This community is important because these are the people who are going to influence you most. When you make a conscious effort to surround yourself with great people, you are going to discover that this will make your transition back into the real world a lot easier. Instead of surrounding yourself with the same crowd, you need to take inventory of what each of these people you were once close to brings to your life currently. If they are not going to be a supportive or positive influence, then you do not need to remain close to them. Cut these ties and make new ones.

People who are going through tough situations need and deserve a positive community, and you are no exception. Whether or not you view it this way, you have just been through a life-changing time where you had to adjust to a completely new way of living. Give yourself credit for this and never forget where you came from. Your inner strength helped you make it through, and you now have the chance to continue your life again. Do not take this time for granted, though, as it is going to be very beneficial to your reentry into society.

Consider going to a support group to meet with like minded individuals. There are support groups for almost any situation you have been through or any vice you are currently grappling with. From addiction to the death of a loved one, other people out there have been through the same experiences. You are not alone, and support groups will prove this to you. When you meet with others who can even remotely relate to the way you feel and what you have experienced, this is going to make it easier for you to open up to them. You just need to see what you have in common.

In support groups, you are going to find a lot of versatility. While not all support groups will include former inmates, you would be surprised at how well you can connect with others just based on other common experiences you have been through. Aside from formal groups that are organized, you can also seek out this same type of support from your loved ones—the more, the better! If somebody wants to support you and has good intentions, then you should take them up on this offer. Try your best to open up to them and to heal from any past experiences that are still haunting you.

The Importance and Benefits of Support Groups

It is going to be challenging to convince yourself that a support group is actually going to be beneficial. You might resist it for some time before you finally work up the motivation to meet other people who have been through very similar experiences. Give yourself time to work your way there, but also keep in mind all of the advantages that can come from being a part of one:

- You will feel less lonely, isolated, and judged. Transitioning back into society after you have been in prison can be rough because you might feel like nobody understands you. This is why being in a support group can help tremendously. You will feel understood and heard. You will always have a place to discuss your feelings and thoughts with a group that has likely felt the same way before. A support group is your judgment-free zone to express yourself and to get advice when you need it. At times, you might also be the one giving advice, which can help you socialize.

- When you talk openly in support groups, you are going to find that your risk of developing anxiety, depression, and stress is significantly lowered. Being unable to vent about what you have been through or what is on your mind is definitely going to cause unnecessary stress in your life, and you need to make sure that you have a proper outlet that you can rely on when times get tough. Even if you feel like life is going all right, it helps to have a group of people with whom you can share your ideas. This is going to keep you feeling motivated.

- Talk openly and honestly about your feelings—this will benefit you in the long run. Not only will you be able to identify what you are feeling, but you will also become a better listener. Make sure that you are listening closely when other people in the support group are talking. It is a great way to learn how to be there for other people.

- Prison is not the only challenge you are going to face in your lifetime. While it is probably the most prominent one that you have experienced lately, you need to prepare yourself for the challenges that have yet to happen. Once they do, you do not need to go through a completely debilitating phase. Make sure that you are prepared for anything and everything by building yourself up from the inside out. When you practice expressing yourself in support groups, you are going to find that it is easier for you to sort through any challenges you might face.

- After your release, you might feel fatigued by chronic conditions. Whether you are ill or just experiencing bouts of insomnia, you still need to remember that these conditions are valid. You have every right to feel like you are worn down from just living your life because this is a huge change that you are still getting used to. The more that you express yourself to your support group, the more normalized your feelings will become. Work through these hardships, and you will start to see results.

How To Find Support

There isn't anything that sounds better than hearing your name being called for R&D (receiving and discharge) over the prison compound speakers. After that, offenders have access to support groups through government agencies or departments, churches or community centers, neighborhood homes, or relief agencies like the St. Vincent De Paul Society and Salvation Army. So, what does life after prison for these returning citizens look like? Will they be able to get affordable housing for a stable and productive reentry?

Housing Services

Housing Services After Prison provides counseling and information on housing support and access pre-release. The goal is to assist individuals in obtaining and maintaining permanent housing.

According to recent statistics, around 50,000 people who are out of prison go directly to a shelter each year, and they are nearly ten times as likely to be homeless. (2020). Most times, this happens because people return to society without a support system, which means no family members or a lack of resources. Let's dive deeper into access tools that can help to find suitable housing after prison release.

- **Affordable Housing:** This is usually privately owned, with the rent being subsidized significantly by the US Department of Housing and Urban Development (HUD). You need to be a low-income senior living with a disability to be eligible for this.

- **Public Housing:** This type of housing is usually owned by the state or local government, paying about 30% of the adjusted monthly income toward rent. Eligibility for this depends on various parameters set by the government that owns the housing. You can find this information from the Public Housing Agency (PHA) in your locality.

- **Private Housing:** This type of housing is the most common: you buy a house or rent it using a traditional lease. While this might cost more than the other options, anyone is eligible to apply.

- **Supportive Housing:** Owned by an organization committed to helping people get permanently housed, this type of housing also includes services to help you. It allows you to build a relationship with your landlord, understand the fundamental rights of a renter, or even help you access the healthcare you need. While eligibility for this depends on your area, you could look out for local organizations that oversee supportive housing. Google "supportive housing [your location]."

- **Transitional Housing:** As suggested, these residences provide you with a stable home while you find permanent shelter. They are otherwise called halfway housing or residential reentry centers. This type of housing also helps you find employment or get the necessary healthcare. Even if they are a bit hard to find, it's worth exploring local options.

Legal Services

The legal services support lawyers who provide legal assistance to convicts and pre-trial detainees (prisoners) concerning the conditions of their confinement and treatment by prison personnel. They do not address issues related to criminal law or procedure, post-conviction remedies, sentencing, parole, probation, immigration detention, or any other forms of civil incarceration.

Here are some of the states with law firms and organizations that provide free legal assistance to people on civil and non-criminal matters: Alabama, Georgia, Kansas, Delaware, Indiana, Minnesota, New Jersey, New York, North Carolina, Nevada, South Carolina, Pennsylvania, West Virginia, and Vermont. There are also national groups that offer to help prisoners by providing legal assistance or high-quality, inexpensive self-help materials. The Prison Law Project has a handbook for prisoners who wish to file a lawsuit per section 1983 in federal court regarding abuse by prison staff or poor prison conditions. The manual also contains information about the American legal system and legal research in general.

Lawyer and an Affordable Legal Aid

Choose a lawyer and legal organizations that give free legal advice, which may also help you find a low-cost attorney. Before looking for an attorney, here are standard fields from which you'd have to decide: criminal law, landlords and tenants, family law, labor, and employment.

Some of the programs that offer a variety of legal aids are:

- Legal Services Corporation (LSC) for people with low incomes.

- Law Help Org for all your legal questions. They offer services for people with low to medium incomes.

- Law Help Interactive for help filling out legal forms, especially those dealing with an uncontested divorce, visitation rights, identity theft, and landlord/tenant disputes.

- American Bar Association for free legal answers. Keep in mind that they will not answer questions that involve crimes.

- Pro Bono Resource Directory finds free legal services in the state.

Legal **Resources for Specific Groups**

For Military and Veterans

- Legal Help for Veterans finds free legal clinics and other necessary resources from the Department of Veterans affairs.

- Stateside Legal finds free legal help for veterans, military members, and their families.

- Armed Forces Legal Assistance finds nearby military installations with assistance offices.

For People with Disabilities

- National Disability Rights Network locates legal service providers by each state for people with disabilities.

For Seniors

- Pension Rights Centre helps people get free legal service for issues with pension, retirement savings plan, or profit-sharing.

- Eldercare Locator can search your state or city's zip code to find local offices focused on legal services and aging.

Employment Services

Many individuals released from prison had a job before their incarceration and want legal and stable employment after release. Specific research on criminal justice suggests that finding and maintaining a job can reduce the chance of former prisoners reoffending or returning to crime. (Petersilia, 2005). However, looking for a job as an ex-prisoner, or any person with a criminal history, could be a daunting experience. Numerous obstacles will stand in your way, but it's not impossible to find the right job. There are so many companies that are "felon-friendly" too.

Here are ways you can begin your job search:

- Make a to-do list that outlines your daily activities

- Apply for jobs early in the day

- Call employers and ask them the best time to apply in person

- Keep track of employers you meet or talk to, including the dates, company and employer names, and notes about your conversations.

- Keep a resume, pen, notebook, and job description handy.

- Follow up immediately, look for leads, and do not wait.

- Let everyone know you're searching for a job.

- Set up job alerts on various job platforms.

Setting Up Your Resume

A resume is a multipurpose tool that highlights all your strengths, abilities, and experiences. Use it to communicate your potential to prospective employers and explain what you can do for them. Be truthful, brief, targeted, and accurate. Write everything positively, limit it to one page if possible, and proofread before sending it across. You needn't emphasize unrelated experiences.

Your conviction can come up if your employer does a background check to confirm your qualifications; hence, be honest with every detail you put into your resume. Overall, keep things simple and make a good impression. Let your employer know what your career goals are and what you aspire to be.

Some online resources (public and private programs) for employment opportunities:

- 2nd Chances 4 Felons is a website that provides links to agencies and companies that hire felons.

- CareerOneStop provides information on exploring careers, finding local help, training, and conducting a job search. It includes a segment titled "Move past your criminal record" and has links to temp agencies and an American JobCentre Finder directory.

- Apprenticeship.gov is a site that provides hands-on-career training information or apprenticeship in areas such as construction, animal care, and welding.

- Disability and Employment is an employment and training administration that provides information for disabled entrepreneurs and workplace accommodations or even information on the Americans with Disabilities Act.

- Career Planning for People With Criminal Conviction is a site that advises on assessing yourself, crafting a career plan, exploring career options, setting goals, expanding skills, and finally finding a job.

- Goodwill is a local organization that can help people connect with employers and build skills and resources to launch their careers.

- Other online sites for ex-prisoners include Employment and Training Administration, Job Accommodation Network, Jobs For Felons, National Reentry Resource Centre, Reentry

Employment Opportunities, Ticket to Work, Restoration Rights Projects, Veteran Readiness and Employment, Women's Prison Association, and so on.

Employment for the justice-involved has been available in the following industries: newspaper delivery, drilling and oil, fast food restaurants and temporary agencies, and online careers.

Support Groups

Support is always available through departments and agencies, at church centers, or in community programs. Neighborhood houses and emergency relief agencies like the St. Vincent de Paul Society also have support groups open 24/7. To find support groups around your locality, you could search the Infoxchange Service Seeker or any national helpline numbers asking for services.

The three largest prison reentry groups are S.O.S.O.L.O., Alternatives to Violence Project, and Marriage After Prison. Apart from these, there are other volunteer groups for ex-prisoners that offer invaluable help. Some of them are partnerships and projects that extend help and support to formerly incarcerated.

Here are some support groups for ex-offenders that allow you to work and volunteer at their organization:

- Action for Prisoners' and Offenders' Families works for the benefit of prisoners by supporting their families.

- North East Prisoner Family Support has been supporting imprisoned people for over 130 years. Providing emotional support, the North East charity supports a positive future for prisoners and their families.

- Ormiston Families Unit Programme serves children and their families through Transforming Rehabilitation Services.

- Out There delivers community-based support (telephone support, mutual support groups, casework including home visits) for families of prisoners.

- Prison Advice and Care Trust, a national charity trust, provides support to people with convictions, prisoners and ex-prisoners, and their families. They help by giving them a fresh start.

- Safe Ground delivers a group that works with people in custodial and community settings. With 21 years of impact, they have flagship programs such as Family Man and Fathers Inside, which are proven to support emotional learning, growth, and development.

- YMCA partners with prisons and supports young offenders with training opportunities and citizenship.

- Women in Prison is a women-run and women-centered organization that provides specialist services to women affected by the criminal justice system.

Service Members and Veteran Support

The Department of Veteran Affairs (VA) provides assistance and a state resource guide for veterans post-incarceration. Any prisoner who has served in the military or National Guard is eligible for help from VA. They get support with compensation, education, healthcare, and housing.

Counseling Services

Prisons and jails in the US incarcerated a large number of people with current or past mental health issues. Several types of research suggest that 37% of people in state and federal prisons have been diagnosed with a mental health problem.

General Practitioner: You must be already registered with your GP in the community where you live. Every prison care team will update the GP on the treatment you've been receiving.

Community Mental Health Team: CMHT gives care and treatment for those with severe mental health issues.

Talk Therapies: A therapist is usually valuable for treating prisoners' mild mental health issues and behavioral problems. Either a GP refers you to a therapist, or you can refer yourself in certain areas. These services are called Improving Access to Psychological Therapies (IAPT), which are provided through National Health Services and are free to use.

Drug and Alcohol Programs

Psychological research proves that treating drug addiction and alcoholism in prisoners during their incarceration and after release helps keep them off drugs and employed *(Inmate Drug Abuse Treatment Slows Prison's Revolving Door, 2004)*.

So, what keeps inmates away from drug problems after their release? "Boot camps" were popular at one time, where substance abuse treatment in prison and after really worked. Substance abuse disorders are treated in various ways in the criminal justice system, such as the following:

- Behavioral therapies such as Cognitive Behavioral Therapy (CBT) that help in modifying the prisoners' use of drugs and the expectations and behaviors associated with them, helping in the effective management of triggers and stress.

- Motivational incentives are given in the form of vouchers or cash to help reinforce positive behaviors.

- Medications such as methadone, naltrexone, and buprenorphine.

- Wrap-around services after release, such as employment and housing assistance.

- Drug Abuse Education: a series of classes that educate prisoners regarding the abuse of drugs and their side effects. These help identify offenders who might need different programming.

- Nonresidential Drug Abuse Treatment is a 12-week Cognitive Behavioral Therapy program that is conducted primarily in groups. It provides insights into criminal lifestyles and skill-building opportunities. Specialized for offenders who have short sentences and are awaiting the Residential Drug Abuse Program (RDAP), transitioning into the community, this program enhances communication skills, community adjustment, and institutionalization.

- Residential Drug Abuse Program (RDAP) is one of the most extensive treatments given to most prisoners. Extending for a duration of nine months, RDAP lets offenders live in a separate unit from the general population, where they participate in half-day programming, half-day work, school, and other activities.

How a Criminal Record Affects Rights of An Ex-Prisoner

A record can affect your ability to move states, get a job, or even vote. It disqualifies you from receiving food stamps, welfare, and public housing, too. Let's take a look at these in detail.

Voting Rights

Most states don't allow incarcerated citizens to vote, and many don't even allow them to vote when on parole or for the rest of their life after conviction. Voting laws vary by state.

Moving Rights

If you are released into a state where you don't wish to live, you can apply for a transfer to another state. If you intend to be there for more than 45 days, then you will need to transfer your supervision to the new state.

Public Housing

People who are convicted of certain crimes that include sex offenses or meth production cannot live in public housing. Your access to public housing can also get denied if you are a drug or alcohol addict who can affect the health or safety of residents.

Child Care Assistance

More than 2.7 million children in the United States have a parent in jail (*Tips to Support Children When a Parent Is in Prison*, n.d.). Often faced with stress, including physical, emotional, academic, or financial hardships, most children struggle to live with the stigma of having a parent incarcerated.

There are several support programs and family-centered services for children whose parents are in prison, which focus on parenting programs, nurturing of family relationships, strengthening activities, community support, and gender-specific interventions.

- State and Local examples include Foreverfamily, a service offering after-school programs, youth workshops, and community projects that address psychological effects of parental incarceration for children, families, and caregivers affected by it.

- The Pathfinder Network seeks to help children whose parents are convicted or involved in the criminal justice system. It supports them with initiatives that create parent leadership and plan changes.

- Hour Children helps women from families affected by incarceration with children and promotes family reunification and reentry into the community.

New Federal Rule on Child Support

Failure to abide by child support can result in incarceration. The Office of Child Support Enforcement (OCSE) published a few rules intended to increase child support programs and enhance their effectiveness. The rules also helped remove barriers in outdated systems to simplify the process of child support. These rules address a few major provisions regarding incarcerated, noncustodial parents.

FAQs on Child Support

1. Can the court order the other parent who isn't in jail to support the child?

Yes, only if the person in jail does not have enough assets or income to raise a child or pay for child support.

1. What if the parent has a child support order but ends up going to jail?

Being imprisoned doesn't change child support automatically unless the judge changes or modifies it. If the incarcerated parent has enough income within the jail, that can be used as child support.

2. What assets does someone in jail have that can be used for child support?

Even if a person is in jail, they might still possess an interest or dividend income from stocks or bonds. They could have rental income, retirement or disability term benefits, money from selling a property, and so on.

Tips to Support Children With Incarcerated Parents

A child can undergo much trauma from stressful events such as their parents being sentenced to imprisonment, yet they thrive by building resilience. The American Academy of Pediatrics identifies having a parent imprisoned as an adverse childhood experience. Here's what can be done for these children:

- Be supportive

- Keep up open communication

- Create a safe space for the child to open up

- Acknowledge and validate a child's concerns

- Encourage active play and skill-building

- Share age-appropriate information with the child and be honest

- Prioritize stability and set up routines

- Involve support adults

- Help the child connect with the incarcerated parent

- Look into child programs that can help, like Temporary Assistance for Needy Families, Medicaid, and so on.

Parenting Skill Programs and Training

The United States prison system offers a variety of parenting programs like Parenting Inside Out for parents who are in the criminal justice system. There is also a community version of this program once parents are released from prison. It has been effective in reducing recidivism and has been shown to improve family relationships and parenting skills.

The Bureau of Prisons (BOP) is another parenting program that provides opportunities for prisoners to bond with children and families. There are other programs that help mothers stay with young children in prison, such as Mothers and Infants Together (MINT) and Residential Parenting Programs (RPP). Parent-child focused programs help prisoners to connect with their family and loved ones; it gives them a positive focus and a reason to get through their imprisonment.

Other means include televisits, where incarcerated parents can visit their children remotely. This entirely depends on the level of security in prison and how much involvement the parents have in their children's lives. In most cases, prisons allow the parents to stay involved with their child's schoolwork. One of the fully secured prisons in New York State will enable mothers to participate in parent-teacher conferences and talk to their children about school problems, homework, and upcoming school events. This way, children feel less lonely without the physical presence of their parents and have the assurance that they are involved and interested in their lives.

Parenting Programs in Correctional Facilities by State

State	Services
Alabama	Family reintegration module that is offered as institutional pre-release/transitional services and reentry program.
Kansas	Parenting classes for offenders Services for non-incarcerated caregivers, play-and-learn groups, workshops, and

State	Services
	transitional support for families
New Jersey	Helping Offenders Parent Effectively (HOPE), offering a 10-week parenting class and support for developing and rebuilding family relationships via Family Reunification and Transition (FRAT)
New Hampshire	Offers a comprehensive array of parenting-focused services associated with Family Connection Centres Parenting classes, support groups, virtual or video visits, parenting libraries, and a chance to be part of several seminars or reading to children

State	Services
Idaho	Parenting programs and six family reunification programs, including Inside Out Dads and Partners in Parenting.
Pennsylvania	Inside Out Dads parenting plans
North Dakota	Three varieties of positive parenting programs
Washington	Programs such as Parenting Inside Out are offered in conjunction with education services, employment, and case management

Mentoring Programs

Prison mentoring programs help alleviate the recidivism rate of a state. Nearly 650,000 people are released from US prisons every year, but their prospects of reentry into a community are quite bleak. The majority struggle without a job or housing because of the lack of a high school education. Close to three-quarters have a history of substance abuse, while one-third suffer from mental health illness or other disabilities.

Volunteer mentors extend valuable support to socially isolated or newly released offenders and act as positive role models. They also work closely with case managers and help the incarcerated people to build skills and improve self-esteem, confidence, and independence. By assisting them in developing and building positive relationships with people in the broader community, community mentor programs aim to improve the offender's ability to cope with all the challenges of living. Ways to find a mentor and other necessary resources are provided in the next chapter.

Domestic Violence Safety Plans

It's always important to think about safety, especially for those with an abusive partner who is about to be released from prison or those who will be returning to an abusive partner on the outside. Most people think the only way out of an abusive relationship is divorce, but there are other means to stay safe even while remaining in partnership. Be sure to use these safety plans with caution without your abusive partner finding it.

Safety Plans at Home

- Keep an extra copy of your keys in a secret place, preferably outside your house.

- Teach your children to call the police or scream for help when they see you being abused.

- Teach your children to stay safe by developing their own plans.

- Develop a code word for safety.

- While arguing, stay away from the kitchen or rooms that have harmful weapons.

- Create an automatic dial on your cell phone to call 911.

- If you need to leave your house, find a safe place you could go to that your partner doesn't know.

Safety Plan If You're Preparing to Leave

- Save a little money every week and keep it hidden from everyone.

- Open a savings account for emergencies.

- Locate the closest phone to your house; it could be at a friend's place or even a payphone. If it's a payphone, then hold on to change.

- Arrange a safe place to stay at any hours.

- Identify domestic violence shelters.

- Keep a bag of clothing and essentials ready at all times.

- Organize and gather all important documents and put them in a locker or any safe place that your partner can't reach and destroy.

- Inform your babysitter, family, neighbors, and friends that your child cannot leave with the partner at any point. If they witness such an abduction, ask them to call the cops immediately.

- Rehearse your escape plan. Practice it with your child.

- Change your PIN numbers and passwords on every social media channel, email, cell phone, and bank statement.

Safety Plan at Work

- Know whom to tell at your work, especially the security personnel.

- Provide a photo of your partner or any perpetrator of abuse.

- If you have an Order of Protection (police report), make sure you share it with your employer.

- If possible, have someone screen your phone calls.

- Use different routes to get to work.

- Keep changing the times you visit a place regularly—for example, grocery stores, churches, or school.

Safety Plan If You're Living Alone

- Change the locks on all doors.

- Install security mechanism at the door.

- Install smoke detectors, fire extinguishers, and window locks.

- Get an Order of Protection.

- Call the cops if your abuser violates this order.

- In rural areas without much visibility, color your mailbox bright red so that your house is easily identifiable.

Digital Safety Planning

The technology that you use is very helpful; however, it can also be used against you. A few things to consider:

- Have you felt that your partner knows too much about your daily activities?

- How comfortable is your partner with technology?

- Do they have access to your social networking accounts or email?

- Do you have a wireless phone or internet access at home?

- Should you check all social media channels you're currently active on for suspicious activity?

Excessive battery drain or a spike in data usage on your phone are indicators that potential spyware or additional software is installed in your cell phone. If possible, try doing a factory reset.

Emergency Relief

In order to effectively help prisoners in times of crisis, there are several proactive emergency measures taken by federal, state, and local governments. Correctional agencies work toward reducing the prison population by providing adequate medical treatment for incarcerated people, hiring correctional staff, and assisting formerly incarcerated people with their transition back into the community.

Some efforts being made at the federal level include the Covid-19 Correctional Facility Emergency Response Act of 2020 (H.R. 6414). However, these protocols and corrections facilities need improvement during national emergencies. The general lack of preparation affects not just the incarcerated but also the surrounding communities. If you're above 65, blind, or have a disability, you will be eligible for social security and income benefits for retirement and disability.

Here are some criteria for eligibility:

- You cannot work as you did before.

- You have a chronic medical condition.

- Your child is under 18 or severely disabled under age 22.

- Your wife is 62 or older and is severely disabled.

Keep Healthy Relationships

The way to continue or begin a relationship after prison life could be stressful and expensive. You might feel that nobody wants anything to do with you or that you've let them down, but it's critical that you (and they) keep communication channels open. Whether short-term or long-term, the prison sentence has several lasting physical and mental effects on the prisoners' lives and families. It's proven, though, that people who have a family and supportive friends outside prison have a better chance of reintegration than those who don't—maintaining regular contact with people you love, then, can help you cope with the daily stress of adjusting to a new life. It keeps you connected and may motivate you to choose a different path in the future. If you know where you want to go, these connections can undoubtedly help you get there.

According to the National Institute of Justice, around 68% of released prisoners get arrested within three years, 83% within nine years. (*National Institute of Justice*, 2020). This shows how ex-prisoners are unable to be successful post-incarceration. Here are a few tips on integrating yourself back into society once your serving period is over.

Find Mentors

A group of mentors or a professional mentor is essential to every inmate for a positive release. Mentors can range from family members and friends to acquaintances or anyone you trust and want to help you. These individuals can undergo training to offer advice, support, and the friendship that ex-inmates need to succeed in life.

Assess Your Strengths and Weaknesses

A person is able to create a framework to accomplish what they want in life when they are able to identify their strengths and weaknesses. Along with pre-release programs, an inmate conducts inventory on themselves. Here, their strengths could be anything from a high school diploma, college, previous employment, or any skill they learned in prison. You could also consider the assets in your life such as social networks and relationships and see how they can impact your life after release.

Recreate Relationships

Redeveloping relationships after release is essential when you reenter society. You need to rebuild and repair your relationship with family and friends to keep you from recidivism. This is possible by keeping in touch through phone calls, letters, or visits.

Serve the Community

Do your best to give back to the society and serve the community after your release. When you contribute your time, effort, and intentionality, you build a constructive future for yourself and others. You could volunteer with various organizations that will help you re-incorporate positive relationships. Carry your skills and areas of expertise to these scenarios and do your best.

Locate Resources

Continue to identify and search for resources well in hand even before your release. Those could be government aids or churches that provide resources for finding food, treatment plans, or anything that comes as a necessity. This will help you release the stress and anxiety that comes with leaving prison.

Start Early

Planning as early as possible for what needs to be done after release is essential. It is one of the most important things to guarantee successful reintegration. Starting early means finding release or pre-release programs or even following up on them. These programs will change your attitude and beliefs about crime, and they also address mental health issues. Additionally, they provide job training and help you find a job post-release.

Chapter 6:
Give Back to Society

Upon release, most prisoners find it difficult to get along with society. The only way is to do your best to serve the community around you, taking time and effort. This helps ex-prisoners build a worthwhile future for themselves. Volunteering at different organizations can reincorporate ex-inmates into the 'new' world they're in and help them build a positive relationship with others.

What Can Volunteering Do For You?

Doing good makes you feel good, and evidence backs this up. Recent research shows that one of the most common negative impacts of incarceration is social withdrawal and isolation. For re-entry into the free world to be successful, former inmates need positive social experiences.

Volunteering Connects You and Others in the Society

Being a member of a network provides a sense of belonging. Volunteering and other face-to-face activities can assist in alleviating loneliness and isolation.

You can connect with people and make the community a better place. Helping others with small tasks can make a huge difference, be it an organization that helps people or an animal welfare center. Volunteering is also a two-way street; your family and friends benefit from it as much as you do. Dedicating some time to this helps you build a positive network and boost your social skills.

Volunteering Is Good, Physically and Mentally

Being kind can boost your self-esteem, happiness, and optimism. It can also help to create a more cheerful atmosphere in the community. When you're in regular contact with people who help you build a solid support system, you can protect yourself from falling into depression. The more you give, the happier you'll feel, and this will, in turn, build your self-confidence.

As a volunteer, you will have a sense of accomplishment and pride. Older adults may feel weak and hopeless; volunteering gives them a purpose and helps them find a direction and meaning in life. It helps a person take their mind off negativity and look at the bright side.

Physical benefits include stress reduction and reduced feelings of rage and animosity, and research shows that helping others might even help us live longer. Your overall psychological well-being improves with a positive connection to animals and people. Such a connection improves your mood and reduces anxiety or other stressors.

Can You Volunteer If You Have a Disability?

Of course you can! People who have chronic health issues or are disabled can significantly benefit from volunteering. In fact, studies show that people with health conditions or other mental health issues benefit from volunteering and show improvement. However, there could also be an initial training session to get you used to the organization and get the hang of the volunteering situation. Make sure there's enough social interaction and the necessary support.

Volunteering Helps You Build Your Career

Giving back to others in need, particularly those who are less fortunate than you, might give you a new perspective. This can help you feel more positive by allowing you to stop focusing on what you think you're lacking. For example, it will enable you to learn essential skills like teamwork, problem-solving, communication skills, task management, project planning, and even work ethics. Once you've honed these skills by volunteering, you can try out for new career positions.

Just because volunteering is unpaid doesn't make it a waste of your skills. Your work can expose you to a professional organization looking for someone with a volunteering background or the necessary skill set you possess. Remember that volunteering is more about the passion and positivity you hold, and the most valuable assets you bring are kindness, compassion, and an open mind.

Finding the Right Volunteering Opportunity

The key to finding the right place to volunteer is to ask yourself the following questions and see if your goals and values align with the organization's needs.

- Who do you want to work with: children, adults, or animals (and in-person or remotely)?

- Are you better suited to a desk job, or do you want to be in the field with a more visible role?

- Do you want to work with a team or alone?

- How much time can you commit?

- What skills do you have that are beneficial for the organization?

- Why is this important for you?

You can also consider looking closely into your goals and interests. Look for something that matches your skills and personality. See if there's something specific that you want to achieve, like improving the neighborhood, meeting people, and expanding your circle, doing something rewarding or trying something entirely different from what you know.

Don't limit yourself to just one place or a specific job; look for more excellent opportunities that are different from what you've explored previously. You can find volunteering opportunities at libraries; community centers, including museums; theatres; service centers, such as rotary clubs and lions clubs; animal shelters; rescue and wildlife organizations; sports teams; youth programs; national parks; conservation or historical restoration programs; churches, synagogues, or any other worship centers; and, finally, online directories or resources like VolunteerMatch, Idealist, National, and Community Service, U.S. Peace Corps, and the American Red Cross.

How to Get the Most out of Being a Volunteer

Volunteering can indeed be time-consuming, and specific tasks can be repetitive. Once you've found the right opportunity, though, considering all the shortcomings such as time, physical limitations, skillset, and interests, there are ways to make the most out of this experience.

- **Ask questions:** Make sure that this experience is right for you by asking your volunteer coordinator the right kind of questions about work, commitments, training, and who you'll be working with.

- **Know what's expected of you:** You must make sure to be comfortable with the organization you work with. You must know what your time and effort goes into. Give yourself the flexibility to make alterations if needed.

- **Don't be afraid to change:** Everything is trial and error, so if you think this organization isn't the right place to grow, you have the freedom to quit. You don't have to be compelled to stick with the same organization for a long time. Find a better fit if necessary and switch.

How to Give Back

Find the Right Mentor

For someone who recently came out of prison, everything could seem new and overwhelming. Imagine the time you had a crisis in your professional or personal life; how did you overcome it? Did you have someone to walk you through this whole crisis and walk in your shoes? That's the role of a great mentor. Mentorship doesn't provide you textbook solutions but just a gentle nudge to lead you in the right direction.

Benefits of Mentorship for Prison Inmates

Mentoring emerged as an approach to help inmates readjust to society. It's great to have someone tell you how they've done things and how you can do it similarly. You might have those skills, or you could be stuck not knowing how.

A study conducted on ex-inmates states that mentored inmates were twice as likely to find a job compared to those who weren't. They also secured a job faster and were more likely to stay on the job for at least three months.

In addition, groups of ex-inmates who had mentors were 35% less likely to re-offend in the following year of their release compared to ex-prisoners who had opted out of the mentoring program.

How to Find a Mentor

You can find the right mentor by checking out the programs you have in your local community. Whether taking part in general volunteering programs or programs specifically made to give ex-inmates a mentor, you can find the right person! How?

- **Look around you:** Other ex-inmates have found mentors in their close circle of friends or family. Find the right influence you need to reenter society the right way. If your best friend is a great role model, consider them as a mentor. Alternatively, if you believe one of your family members can give you the mentorship that you need, seek their help.

- **Professional Network:** Your current workplace is another place to search. Many peer relationships have ended in long-lasting friendships where you can reach out for career advice, interview tips, job opportunities, and a lot more. Look at everyone at your workplace as a potential mentor, like peers you've attended college with or members of professional groups that you're involved in. There could be a manager you looked up to or a friend who's doing a remarkable job. It's not just easier to approach these people; they may also be more receptive to your request.

- **Online Network:** Online communities are a fantastic place to meet your potential mentors. Since it's all virtual, it's immediate, and you can search out a repertoire of advice on every conceivable topic. No matter how active you are, be a part of social media platforms like LinkedIn, Slack, Quora, Reddit, or Twitter. Find people who share their experiences, spend time helping others, and engage in discussions. If your mentor has a blog, follow what kind of content they share. If you find someone offering helpful advice online, the chance is good they could also be doing it offline in person.

- **Share Your Learnings:** As you know the difficulty of finding a mentor online, it's imperative to share your learning with others who need it. People appreciate when you do this and will reach out to you for more information. This can develop a co-mentorship, where you're both helping each other with each of your own experiences.

- **Be Proactive:** Take more initiative, and instead of being an onlooker, be a doer. This way, a potential mentor is more likely to notice you. Volunteer, start side projects, or use your skills to help people in your community.

Ways to Secure a Meaningful Mentorship

- **Know What You Need and Stay Committed:** Once you are aware of what you want from a mentor, you can begin searching for one. This is much like finding a job opportunity that aligns with your goals, dreams, and aspirations. You just have to find the right person who will help you. Do not get distracted—commit yourself to finding the right mentor. Ask questions like: Do I associate with the right people? Will this person add value to my life? Do I belong in this networking group? Am I being challenged enough? How did other people find their mentors? This will help you get on the right track, so be committed and open your mind to new possibilities.

- **Don't Only Talk About Work:** Simply discussing work, even with a colleague, could be a boring discussion. Instead, spend more time understanding each other's personal views, choices, and priorities. Make your conversations more interesting by discussing your aspirations and dreams, how you like to spend weekends, and work-life balance. Keep the conversations light and candid.

- **Be Responsible and Invest in Your Mentor:** Once you know your needs, begin exploring all kinds of mentors. Learn to be vulnerable and honest with yourself. Be thoughtful when you look for a suitable person. Invest your time and resources in finding the person who is clear, focused, and responsible.

- **Set an Agenda and Meet Regularly:** A meeting that's scheduled will only work when both of you are prepared. Send your discussion points in advance to your mentor so that they can be prepared. Focus on a few things and don't expect them to find a solution to all of them. Instead, allow your mentor to share their experiences and help you find a solution for it yourself. Meeting regularly will ensure you both don't lose touch with each other. It's also the best way to measure progress and track your goals.

- **Be Accountable to Others and Yourself:** In other words, share your hard work and progress, and do not be selfish. Your mentor is someone who helps you progress in your career. Mentoring means monitoring your progress, and if you slip, a mentor starts to reevaluate the time they commit to this relationship.

- **Create Opportunities for Your Mentor and Be Selfless:** Making the mentor-mentee relationship work will require you to create new opportunities for your mentor equally. It represents the two sides of the same coin. Make sure you create opportunities for each other. Be selfless, listen, and think of ways you can add value to your relationship. You could also buy them a book, connect them with another friend, or send them a link to an article. This way, your mentoring relationship can last a lifetime.

- **Create a Lasting Relationship:** This could be more difficult than you think; as time passes, so does your life, and the desire to find a new mentor could become apparent. Our lives keep evolving and need change; however, the mentor who helped you grow and reach where you are today shouldn't be ignored. It could be that you have outgrown the need for your current mentor; however, the relationships you've made from the previous chapters of your life must remain. You need to set the expectations to manage your relationship effectively. Be accountable and act responsibly to cultivate a mutually beneficial partnership.

How to Approach Potential Mentors

When you've found your mentor, you could get tempted to fire an email ASAP asking them to mentor you. But, building a friendship before asking for mentorship goes a long way. You could ask them if they're fine with meeting you a couple of times to better get to know each other. Leave thoughtful replies under their content to get their attention and start a conversation. Remember that your potential mentor could be receiving hundreds of messages and emails every day, so you aren't exceptional. The key is to get them to notice you and remember you from a pile of cold email requests. Hence, building your relationship is a significant advantage.

What to Look for in Mentorship

Your partnership isn't going to be fruitful if your mentor is not the right person. A mentor can't be just anyone, so here are a few things to consider when evaluating a prospective mentor:

- Both your career paths should align

- They must possess the qualities, skills, business acumen, endurance, knowledge, and willingness to be your mentor.

- Their advice must be actionable.

- They must be available and attentive. It's pointless to approach someone who is busy running two companies. They will not have the time to commit to you.

Finally, it's essential to respect your mentor for who they are. Check for qualities that matter to you and see if they maintain a work-life balance. Make sure their priorities match yours to help build the rapport between the two of you.

Ways to Give Back to the Society

Giving back to your community can bring you miles closer to your goals, be they big or small. It makes a huge difference when you're volunteering or donating money to someone in need. Indeed, it has a positive impact not just on the person on the receiving end, but also the giver. The art of giving is also known as philanthropy, which has been around since the dawn of humanity. It helps to eliminate social problems and increases the well-being of society. We might think that our efforts aren't paying off, but what if all of us did the same? One person alone might not save the world, but all of us together can. Our part could be something as minor as doing grocery shopping for your old neighbor.

Here are simple ways you can give back to the community and create a positive impact on others' lives:

Donate Your Time

Time is precious, and allocating it to the area that needs it is way more valuable. One of the most fruitful ways you can do this is to volunteer at places like animal shelters, NGOs, schools, and shelters for homeless people. Start small during your free time, and you'll soon realize how much you love volunteering.

Support Local Farmers

Shop at your local farmers' stand or market to give back for all the hard work that farmers in our community do for us. Even if you only buy fresh produce there, you will directly support their business.

A Random Act of Kindness

Even simple acts of kindness can help enhance your area when you volunteer with your time and energy. A charitable deed such as lending a helping hand to a neighbor who is balancing a bag of groceries or lifting a piece of furniture makes a lasting impression.

Donate Blood

The gift of life is the greatest gift of all. It only takes an hour to provide this valuable resource and save lives during a medical emergency.

Be a Part of Charity Events

Join a charity or a helpful organization and volunteer as a listener, a healthcare champion, or a peer supporter.

Finding a cause you care about can be a powerful motivator for volunteering at or even organizing a fundraising event or philanthropic activity in your neighborhood.

Organize a Community Clean-Up

You can gather a group of people to clean up a garden, pick up litter, paint park benches, build a house for the homeless, pull weeds, and so on. Making your neighborhood more welcoming will bring great praise from society.

Donate Your Clothes or Any Unwanted Items

This is one of the best and easiest ways to give back to the community. You must have clothes that don't fit you or any accessories/stationeries that you no longer use, like Homegoods. This method is also budget-friendly because you are giving things you already own and not buying new things. The best items to donate are clothes, shoes, hygiene products, baby care items, and non-perishable food.

Help a Child in Need

Volunteering at organizations to help a child or improve the lives of youth in foster care is an excellent way to start. These organizations are continually on the lookout for volunteers; they also help youths who have aged out of the foster care system by providing resources.

Volunteer at a Senior Center

Volunteering at your local senior center as a way to give back to the community can help certain seniors avoid feeling isolated and depressed. You may help by assisting elders with everyday duties while ensuring that they remain independent and in their own homes. You can also help aging seniors by volunteering with organizations that benefit seniors in need.

Plant a Tree

Times have changed, and the environment is at stake. Air pollution is a significant concern, but with each tree that's planted, we can reduce the toxicity in the environment. This, in turn, boosts the overall wellbeing of our ecosystem.

Set Up a Volunteer Day

Several companies encourage their employees to participate in a not-for-profit organization, enabling their staff to take a day off to volunteer. You could arrange or be part of an annual, quarterly, or monthly volunteer day.

Share Ideas and Abilities

Start a program that's affordable for your community, like teaching or art classes. Assist kids or the elderly with guides on basic things like household fixes. If you're a writer, help a charity with their press release. You could even play guitar for others, teach kids on your day off, or start gardening in your neighborhood.

Get Into Recycling

When discarded materials, such as plastics and paper, are recycled, they turn into new items. This is incredibly beneficial to the environment and decreases the consumption of natural resources and pollutants. Offering money in exchange for recycling at your local recycling facility is a nice bonus that you can utilize for community service.

Become a Mentor for Other Ex-Convicts

We're sure that during your time in prison, you must have made some connections. Sometimes, these friends and acquaintances will need someone to help them reenter society once they are out of jail. You can take this opportunity to teach another ex-convict a skill you have, such as model-making, guitar playing, or literacy. You can even help them with housing and volunteering, showing them the way you are reentering society now.

Promote Causes on Social Media

It's all right if you can't support these causes directly; that doesn't mean your circle can't. Sharing these causes on your social media platforms can spread the word and bring more attention to them. Promote community fundraisers, drives, or events that you feel need more assistance. You might not know who else could learn of or share this from your profile.

Chapter 7:
Get Back Into Education

People who serve time in jail are denied educational chances for the rest of their lives, making it practically impossible to obtain the credentials they need to prosper following their release. Even if they are eager to return to their community and get back to work, the reality is an uphill battle. Recently, incarcerated people have lacked the opportunity to obtain a high level of education due to issues such as the school-to-prison pipeline, making it extremely difficult to have a thriving career.

According to a survey by the Prison Policy Initiative, more than half of individuals who have been released from prison have only a high school diploma or GED, and a quarter have no credentials at all, contributing to a 27 percent unemployment rate among those who have been released (Writers, 2020).

Education is critical for people seeking employment, especially after their prison tenure. Here are some facts about formerly incarcerated people and their educational attainment:

- Previously imprisoned people are nearly twice as likely to have no high school credential at all.

- More than half of ex-inmates hold only a high school diploma/GED, which have less value in the current job market.

- Unlike the public, people who have been imprisoned are more likely to have GEDs than traditional high school diplomas.

- Three-quarters of GED certificates are earned in prison.

Formerly imprisoned individuals are eight times less likely to complete college than the general public.

Federal Programs for People With Criminal Background

Work Opportunity For Tax Credits (WOTC)

WOTC is a federal program that targets those from certain groups facing significant barriers to employment, which includes those who have been convicted. The credit is paid as an incentive to the employer for giving an opportunity to a person from this targeted group to work. This is a great way to earn some tax credits and help your reentry run smoothly.

The Federal Bonding Program

Providing fidelity bonds for 'at-risk' job seekers, the federal bonding program covers the first six months on the job, which will be at no cost to the employee or employer. As protection against fraudulent or dishonest acts, the bond serves as a "safety net" for the employer.

Fair Chance Pledge and Fair Chance Employers

As part of an Obama-era initiative, the Fair Chance Pledge is taken by employers across the nation. It aims to reduce and eliminate barriers to reentry into the workforce. Employers or organizations that pledge agree to promote fair hiring processes like delaying criminal history questions towards the end of the hiring process or ensuring that job training is provided to those with criminal records.

What to Do Before You Apply for Schools

If you've recently been out of prison, then you must be ready to apply for a school or job right away. However, here are a few pieces of paperwork that need to be done before this.

Get an ID or Driver's License: The majority of the time, a person's driver's license has expired by the time they are released. They can recover the license for a modest charge, or they may have to retake the test if it has been a specific number of years since the last time they took it. For some prisoners, their license could have been revoked due to the crime they committed, such as a felony DUI. In this case, they will need to petition the court to reinstate the license. If it's just a matter of issuing the license, you'll be walked through the procedure at the local county courthouse. If it's a reinstatement of a revoked license, it is much more challenging and needs the services of an attorney. Having an official ID or driver's license can give you a leg-up in society when you apply for schools. They will often be required during your application process.

Get a Permanent Address: In many states, obtaining a driver's license or another form of identification necessitates proof of a permanent residency. A utility bill at that particular address in your name, a fellow resident filing an affidavit, or a copy of the lease agreement confirming you live at the residence are all examples of proof of permanent presence. Depending on the rules of the school you plan to apply to, they likely require a permanent address to be able to send you the documents you need throughout your school years. If this might be tough for you to do as soon as you get out, ask for help! You have friends and family that love you and want to help you; consider talking to them and using their addresses in case you need it. Establishing a permanent address can take a couple of weeks to months, depending on the rules of the agency you're working with.

Study the Transportation System: Without a vehicle, getting to and from school can be challenging. Check out the local bus lines, trains, subways, and other public transportation options. Many areas have taxi companies that operate 24 hours a day, seven days a week. You could also choose to buy or borrow a vehicle from a friend or family member.

Meet All Court-Ordered Requirements: There are likely some court-order requirements that you have to look into upon release. These include counseling sessions, meeting the parole officer, or anything along similar lines. The requirements will have a time period to clear them, so look at the paperwork you were given upon release. Contact your attorney, parole officer, or anyone you know at the court for help if you aren't sure of something.

Get a Phone Number: Having a phone number where schools can reach you is vital to getting an education or a job. Since cell phone plans can be expensive, consider getting on a plan with a family member. You could also use some other form of phone services, such as Skype or any messenger services.

Consider Counseling: Most individuals who are out of prison can find it hard navigating through the education system because of their history. Luckily, schools and organizations provide counseling sessions that will help you get back on your feet. It's essential to find the right kind of counselor or join a support group to keep you from relapsing. You could even contact your local division for social services and learn about community programs for referrals to a professional counselor or social worker.

Get Healthcare Coverage: Finding out a way to pay for healthcare can be challenging for a formerly incarcerated individual. This is crucial, though, for those who have a medical condition and are in need of regular treatment or medications. The Affordable Care Act will help you find your eligibility for a subsidized health care plan and your coverage. You could also speak to the customer care service representative to learn what other options are available. The Department of Human Services (DHS) is an excellent place to start.

Financial Aid and Scholarships for People With a Criminal Background

Scholarship	Amount	Eligibility	Application
Federal Work-Study	Varies	Offered to students in financial need, allowing them to work part-time on campus	Fill out the FAFSA form to determine whether you are qualified.

Scholarship	Amount	Eligibility	Application
		Eligible for people who were formerly incarcerated in a federal or state institution	
Federal Supplemental Educational Opportunity Grant	100 USD to 4000 USD a year	Awarded to undergraduate students Awarded to those who are also eligible for Pell Grants	Application FAFA is the only way to apply
Employment and Training Administration Grants	Varies	The division of the Department of Labor authorizes grants to those who	Approach your local college or school for this particular grant and ask if this is

Scholarship	Amount	Eligibility	Application
		are seeking reentry after imprisonment. They provide local community opportunities.	possible and, if so, if you are eligible.
Scholarships	Varies	This varies, but there are several options that don't ask for criminal history. Schools like Adams State University or Wheaton College offer scholarships, particularly for formerly incarcerated	Fill out FAFSA and check your potential school or college for a scholarship opportunity. While seeking scholarships, pay attention to rules, and if they don't mention background checks or criminal

Scholarship	Amount	Eligibility	Application
		people.	records, then you might qualify.

Education Programs and Job Planning Resources

Back in 1986, 25% of adults who were out of prison didn't have a high school credential while low-skill jobs were still available, and decades later, it's getting harder for former inmates to compete with a skilled labor market (Initiative, n.d.-a) Hence, there's no reason for former prisoners to wait to get a jumpstart on their education or workforce. Inmates can take advantage of job planning resources and several education programs before they move into their community.

GED programs: These are pretty common in prison, with at least 70% of state or federal inmates earning their GED while incarcerated. Research has also identified essential benefits of in-prison GED programs, which include reduced recidivism and higher post-prison earnings. In addition, for inmates who do not have a high school diploma, GED programs help to bridge the educational gap.

Free Educational Programs: Apart from GED, there are other programs like literacy classes, wellness education, or library services that enhance new knowledge and skills in inmates.

Vocational and Technical Training: Certain prisons provide you with hands-on technical experience and training that can boost your resume upon release. This can help with entry into a qualified profession.

College Classes: For inmates who are in facilities that don't provide an onsite college-level curriculum, the best way to earn a college credit or degree is through distance correspondence courses. Some offer correspondence courses for all, and others offer only to specific students who are in the correctional system.

Career Counseling: Parolees might require a group setting or a one-on-one session with a professional counselor.

Benefits of Education for Previously Incarcerated People

Access to higher education is deprived for formerly incarcerated (FI) people when compared to the general population. The disparities in this are widely caused by institutional barriers that prevent ex-inmates from accessing further education. However, educating FI individuals has several benefits, increasing civic engagement, supportive social networks, and economic opportunity. In order to expand these opportunity curves for FIs, policies are needed to develop and establish support programs and eliminate college application barriers, transitional barriers, and secondary education funding.

Civic Engagement

When higher education is easily accessible to formerly incarcerated people, there is an increased civic engagement, with more and more FI people becoming aware of felony oppressive systems like prison industrial complex and income inequality. Additionally, FI individuals develop the necessary skills to address discriminatory policies and practices that negatively impact them by recognizing these.

Apart from this, FI people who are educated further engage civically by voting (if given the right). Forty-eight states in the US allow ex-prisoners to vote with restrictions. Vermont and Maine are exceptions where the citizens never lose their right to vote even when in custody.

Economic Opportunities

Economic security is one of the most important benefits of higher education. While research on this is scarce, an internal revenue service study found that only half of FI people gained employment within a year of release. Out of those who gained employment, their average salary was less than those with minimum wages (Acevedo, 2020)

Although ex-prisoners with a degree might still face barriers to employment, having a degree has been shown to raise their chances of being employed with a higher pay.

Social Networks

With higher education comes a group of people who can guide and work with you to find careers, get access to resources, and do better in life. Finding the right kind of support group and community is an essential benefit of secondary education for FI individuals. Additionally, while pursuing a higher education, they also have the potential to create a transformative change in their lives and communities. Most formerly incarcerated students describe their academic year as a central part in overcoming adversity in their personal lives. Students gain access to mentoring programs, research projects, student organizations, and a lot more, empowering them to ultimately open new doors to ideas and opportunities that would otherwise be closed.

Tips for Getting Hired

Most people who were involved with justice in the past had one question: "Who will ever hire me?" but the truth is, there are several companies out there that are looking for someone with your potential.

Work on Your Networking Skills: Networking should begin way before you've been released. Talk to parole or correctional officers and counselors or anyone who might be able to put a good word on your behalf. After release, take advantage of these resources and network with them all.

Know Your Rights: While employers can ask for a background check, they cannot discriminate against you during hiring using that information. Employers must seek permission before checking your history and should give you a copy of the report. You are also eligible to receive a summary of your rights and notice if you aren't hired based on the report.

There are several states adopting the "Ban the Box" laws, which basically prohibits employers from asking a potential candidate's background or history until an offer is made.

Create a "Why Should I be Hired?" List: You've learned a lot from your legal troubles, and you know you've changed since then. It's time to lead a better life and set an example to others by striving for success. You could put a few points like these in your list and think of various other reasons why you should be hired.

Learn a Few Basics of the Interview Process: It's essential to brush up on all your basics, like arriving on time, shaking hands, smiling, and saying hello. Dress well and always maintain good eye contact. Remember to thank your interviewer at the end of your session.

Always answer all your questions honestly—this will make a great impression.

Be Easily Contactable: Make sure to check your email and attend calls regularly.

Don't Give Up: The road to permanent employment is indeed challenging. You need to remind yourself that every employer who passes your application allows you to find something even better. Stay focused, and don't give up.

Frequently Asked Questions

1. Where can I find a college and financial aid applications?

If you need help with financial aid and admissions, there are officers for the same who help potential students regardless of their prior records. You could also approach a social worker, probation or parole officer, or advocacy groups for help.

1. Is it necessary to disclose criminal history in college applications?

If asked, it's always best to be truthful, and policies will depend on each school. A criminal history needn't always lead to automatic disqualification. There should be schools that are open to admitting formerly incarcerated individuals.

1. Can I still live on-campus?

This again depends on the school and the type of your conviction. Most schools conduct background checks on every student living on campus. If certain convictions could disqualify you from living on campus, see what can be done. If not, always have a backup plan for living arrangements.

1. How will I pay for college tuition?

There are certain restrictions for incarcerated people; however, most of them will be lifted upon their release. Check out the school's financial aid and scholarship funds to learn more.

1. How will I adjust and avoid a relapse into criminal behaviors?

This is a widespread concern among incarcerated individuals; it shows that they are determined not to make the same mistake. You can seek help from many sources, like support groups, on-campus mental health centers, counseling services, and so many more. It's always best to be open with the college staff and faculty for any support that you may need. They will ensure you get help in time.

Chapter 8:
Say Goodbye to Negative Influences

Prison relationships also have challenges attached to them which aren't just financial issues, but also losses of trust. The longer someone stays incarcerated, the less trust they have for people. It's a part of being sentenced to prison, and you quickly learn to trust no one. However, trust is an essential factor for a positive and healthy relationship after prison life; it's necessary to function once you're out from behind bars. Remember that healthy relationships have boundaries, but they are supposed to broaden your world and not narrow it. Whether you are going to be set free or you have a loved one heading home soon, you will have to pay attention to re-developing relationships.

Tips for Maintaining the Trust and Having a Healthy Relationship with Yourself and Others If You've Been in Prison

You might go through culture shock: Depending on how long you've been in prison, one of the most significant challenges to re-entry is culture shock. There could be new technology, the rise of social media, cultural norms, new versions of gadgets, and life organization or development. It could take a while to get adjusted to the new normal.

Be Aware of Depression: It's common to suffer from mental health illness when you're in prison or after. Working toward finding a job (especially with a criminal record), readjusting to life, building healthy relationships, and gaining stability in life can all be frustrating. You can start with small goal setting or work with a loved one together, or even practice self-talk. If there is no improvement, consider reaching out for professional help. Treat yourself to a modest reward once each goal is fulfilled, such as a long walk or a special lunch. The more success you achieve, the more you'll find yourself avoiding negative habits.

Find Someone to Motivate You: You might be surrounded by negative thoughts such as "I can't do this" or "I will never find a job." Find someone to give you positive affirmations so these negative influences seem minor to you.

Don't Go Back to Your Old Habits: You have probably made some tough choices because of negative influences that have landed you in prison in the first place. Dealing with these habits and avoiding them is the first thing you need to do. If your neighborhood is riddled with crime, it's time for a change of habit. If your friends negatively influence you and encourage you to commit crimes, it's time for a change. Study what is going on in your life, make the changes you need to make, and get your life back on track.

Dealing with Anger and Frustration: Incarceration can change a person, as anger and aggression are methods of protection in prison. The best way to improve your relationship when you have anger management issues is through communication. Find a middle ground and keep accountable to improve your communication: practice mindfulness and other relaxation techniques to control your emotions.

Focus on Communication: When these negative thoughts are in your mind, pushing you to fall back into your old habits, communication is the best way to get them out of your head. Find someone you can talk to as much as possible. When you feel the sudden urge to fall back into your old habits, find the right person to let out your frustrations to. Communication is the most effective technique to alleviate frustration. Finding a happy medium and maintaining accountability will keep the lines of communication open and improve your communication.

Handling Rejection: Rejection is something that comes in many forms, be it from your employer, friends, family, or partner because of the stigma they associate with incarceration. Remember to go easy on yourself. You cannot change people, but you can change the way you choose to react to rejection. Learn to move on and continue to improve your circumstances. Remind yourself that you aren't a failure and stay focused. Give yourself credit for progress.

Encourage yourself to focus on your ultimate desired outcome rather than your past failures.

Stay Away From Negative Influences and Combat Addiction: Be aware of what's negative and discuss your comfort levels and individual restraints. Stick to what you feel is right by understanding your needs and goals. If you're unsure, talk to someone. Addictions can be challenging to work through if you have no support. If it gets complicated, find a therapist who can provide you with the necessary treatment to combat addiction.

Tips for Maintaining a Healthy Relationship If Your Loved One Is an Inmate

Assess the Feasibility of Your Relationship: One of the most brutal truths about having a partner in prison is that it's more complex and demanding than other types of relationships. This is not to discourage you but to encourage a pragmatic relationship. Be prepared for a long-distance relationship, even if you're in the same city as your partner's prison. Ask yourself if the lack of physical contact is something you can deal with.

Don't Send Them Money Continuously: Make sure your relationship isn't based on monetary lines. Since prisoners are deprived of luxuries, they may rely on their friends or family for money. Occasional expenditure sounds fine, but make sure it's not a repeated affair. On the other hand, you must be preparing them to face real-world problems (finding a job or shelter) once they're out of prison.

Try and Visit Them on Their Holidays: Apart from the weekly or monthly visits, try and visit them on occasions such as Christmas, Easter, or New Year's. These days make prisoners feel lonelier than the rest, and it also reminds them of the beautiful times they had before being incarcerated.

Give Surprise Visits: Time in prison heavily affects relationships, and if you want a successful reintegration, revisiting these connections is crucial. Usually, inmates know when you will visit them as a part of your regular visits; however, when you give them a surprise visit, it means a lot to them.

Introduce Them to Your Friends: Just like in regular life, you need to introduce your partner in prison to your friends outside. As your friends know you well, meeting your partner gives you a new perspective into your relationship. A second opinion from a trusted friend is always helpful.

Talk About Your Life Goals: You can learn a lot about a person from their life goals and aspirations. It's always essential to have a person who is on the same wavelength, especially when they are an ex-prisoner. Understanding each other on a more intellectual level ensures a healthy relationship.

Rebuilding and repairing relationships with family and friends can be the aspect that keeps someone from recidivism. Begin this relationship work before release as well with letters, telephone calls, and visits. Starting before you get out can help you navigate life after you're released.

Ways to Overcome Negative Influences

Most situations and acts that we come across every day are either influenced by something or someone. To influence means to have an effect on a person's thoughts or actions and everything that they do or say. Now, influence could be both positive and negative; when you are negatively influenced, you tend to do all wrong things. However, we can overcome bad influences in the right ways.

Setting Boundaries: Negative influence can happen even when it's something we didn't choose. You must know when to step back or say 'NO,' whether you are in your workspace, at school, or on social media. Know what is best for you and avoid getting into relationships that raise red flags. Promptly leaving a conversation or blocking people from your life will help you avoid harm.

Good Values and Morals: We've all been taught values at a very young age, so do not let bad influence overpower your values. Negativity is like the flu, and once it catches you, it gets a bit challenging to get rid of it. Don't let people into your circle if their values and morals don't align with yours. When you are self-aware, you can be sure if someone is worthy of being your friend; if not, say goodbye.

Combat Negative Thinking: As they say, you are your thoughts. If you do not cut negativity from your mind, or if you have a negative image of yourself, you're always going to attract negativity from the outside. Avoid people that reinforce these negative thoughts or make you feel any lesser. Set goals and aims in life and try to achieve them. Look deeply into yourself to find your positives and work toward being a better person.

Avoid Bad Influences on Social Media: Not just in person, it's also essential to follow the right kind of people online. The pages you follow and the people you look upon must have a positive influence on you. Unfollow or block people online if you think they are toxic or spread hate. You could also report the pages and spread the message. Take the right step to cut out someone who is neglectful, uncaring, or abusive.

Get Organized: A great way to say goodbye to negativity is to get organized. Start with your bedroom; the more simple things are to find around your bedroom, the less time you spend looking for something. Sleeping in a clean and uncluttered space reduces stress and gives you a restful sleep. A disorganized space, in contrast, leads to a muddled mind that doesn't allow you to focus. So, think minimalistic and start getting organized.

Do One Good Thing Every Day: Doing something well doesn't always have to be monetary. You could save a kitten from a drain or help your neighbor water his garden, pick your niece from school, smile at a stranger, or do some grocery shopping for a sick person. Do something nice and unexpected every day for people around you.

Remember You Are Loved: If you lack self-love or think nobody loves you, you look for love in all the wrong places. This may lead you to the wrong person or the wrong group. It's important to mend your relationships with others and yourself without being insecure and feeling unloved.

Learn to Say No: A 'no' is always a 'no' and never a 'maybe.' The power of NO is irreplaceable, and you won't realize it until it uses it wisely. It takes a lot of courage to say no to people who could be your friends or close family members, but you must learn to say NO when something is against your morals or values or if you simply disagree with a person.

Try and Be Independent: The person you are dependent on could be the one who's badly influencing you, and you have no choice but to stay. However, you don't have to stay if it's affecting you mentally; try and find a way to be independent and take care of yourself. When you're wrongly influenced by the person you're dependent on (this could be your parents or spouse) you give up thinking there's anything you can do. But that needn't be the case forever; you have plenty of opportunities to work for yourself and earn a living. Do not let someone control you; instead, break away from them and find your solace elsewhere.

Communicate: Communication is the key to everything. To overcome negative influences, it's always best to understand a person's behavior, know what changed them, and communicate your thoughts. If you're the one who needs help, then seek a therapist and resolve your negative thoughts or influence by communicating. If you find someone struggling with a negative impact, listen to them. At times, being a good listener goes a long way, and you can see that many times people who fight negative influences just want someone to hear them out.

Move Your Body: It's scientifically proven that doing physical exercise like yoga, jogging, or even going for a walk can make you feel better both physically and mentally. When your physical body becomes fit, you tend to be more self-confident, which in turn helps you overcome insecurities. Meditating and breathing exercises are also great ways to combat negative influences and find inner peace.

Personality Development Course: People who are easily negatively influenced are those who are insecure about themselves. To become intensely aware of what's right and wrong, personality development classes help people identify their strengths and weaknesses. It makes them better humans and helps them overcome bad influences.

Learn to Ignore: If you don't want to directly tell someone that they are a negative influence on you, learn to ignore them. You are not liable to answer calls or meet them. Connections are meaningful, but if they are badly influencing you, it's always better to let go. Find new people in life. Make new connections at a coffee spot or in communities like youth programs or sports academies.

You Can Always Make New Friends: A lot of people stay in toxic relationships because they are afraid to let go of their so-called friends, thinking they will never find friendship again. The moment you realize you can't have fun, relax, or be yourself around a person, it's time to move on. Cutting a relationship off doesn't mean blocking out your friend's circle. Be patient; the right person will always come to you and stay.

Reasons Why It's Time to Say Goodbye to Negativity

1. **Negativity Eats You Alive:** It's true that you cannot always let a negative thought just pass by, but unchecked negativity will stay in for longer and start to become debilitating. It's going to eventually captivate your mind, and it's going to be challenging to reverse this.

2. **Negativity Spreads:** Entertaining your negative thoughts or circles for long can alter your personality, which eventually spreads to your close friends and family. Whether you speak or listen, your body language, facial expression, and tone rub off on those around you.

3. **Negativity Debilitates:** When you let negativity captivate your mind, you basically say goodbye to productivity. Dwelling on negative thoughts could make you stare at your screen for hours. Even when you know it's a waste of time, it gets hard to break the vicious cycle.

4. **Negativity Is a Choice:** Well, not always, but most of the time, you choose to hear or see what you want. Most of the time, these are situations that are under your control and which you can avoid.

Chapter 9:
Adjust to New Routines

Prison changes people, and so a routine will be quite beneficial when you're finally outside. Your time in prison is not your own. What you do during the day is well planned. This means that having the freedom to do whatever you want with your leisure when you're in prison seems like heaven. It's a thrilling experience, but it's also a very stressful one when you come out because you're used to having meal times pointed out. Sometimes, people forget to eat for an extended period of time or grow concerned about the amount of free time they've been given.

Around 10000 prisoners are released from state and federal prisons every week in the United States. About 650,000 of them each year; unfortunately, two-thirds of them end up back in prison within three years. (*SFGATE*, 2019) This is likely because ex-convicts face a lot of challenges outside the prison and cannot get their feet on the ground and build a new life. A daily routine will help you calm down when you're fresh out of prison. It is not necessary for your regimen to be elaborate.

The Importance of a Schedule

Actively establishing a schedule can help you keep your work-life balance. It enables you to prioritize every need efficiently and support productivity. It also gives you satisfaction as an ex-inmate because you feel accomplished doing things on your own. Other benefits of having a schedule include meeting all your daily goals, limiting procrastination, and establishing a healthy lifestyle. Once you have gotten out of prison, complete your goals, such as enrolling in a school, getting a job, getting an ID, and getting back out there.

A routine will help make sure you keep things on track, that your life has a purpose, and that you are sticking to the same frequency of activities. Not only will this help you reenter society, but it will also keep you away from habits that you aren't proud of. This is the final step in getting your life back together.

So, here are several ways you can adjust to your life outside prison.

Start Slow

Don't expect to adapt yourself to a new routine immediately. This is a painful and time-consuming process that could discourage you, but rather than focusing on how soon you can finish a task, focus on how better you can do it even when it takes time. Start with something as simple as waking up at the same time in the morning. You can then add new habits one by one once you've accomplished this. This will help you avoid feeling overwhelmed.

Write Everything Down

Begin by writing down all your tasks, both professional and personal. You could either do this weekly or daily. Don't edit or organize; rather, focus on brainstorming. Don't forget to include household tasks like changing sheets or doing laundry, as these are also time-consuming.

Learn What's Changed

There's a good chance that things have significantly changed if you've been in prison for quite some time. You must have gone to jail before all the transitions happened, and henceforth, you'll need to learn what has changed after you were incarcerated. Ask friends and family for help and guide you through these changes.

Prioritize

Once you've made a list, identify your priorities and mark them from most important to least. Use a highlighter to organize them visually; this is very appealing and encourages you to do those tasks. Organize them as work, personal, and others. For example, you could highlight personal tasks like making breakfast and doing laundry in yellow, while work tasks like answering calls and replying to emails can be in blue. You could underline others like going out for a coffee with a friend in pink.

Create Smaller Tasks

These can be menial things like doing the dishes, going for a walk in the morning, or setting a meal schedule. Make sure you have these. Remember, you were told when to eat in prison and didn't have to worry about making the food. This time, you do. Find what eating schedule works well for you and stick to it.

Make a Weekly and Daily Plan

Your daily plan can be things to do around the house. Your weekly plan needs to be broader goals that you want to accomplish throughout the week. It could be studying for a class you are taking or getting some errands done when you are trying to reenter society. It could be getting your ID or driver's license, speaking at schools, finishing your CV, and applying to jobs.

Be Flexible with Your Tasks

It's okay to change your routine every now and then. The whole purpose of creating your routine is finding what works for you. If you don't like walks in the morning, change it. This is a trial-and-error process that will help you establish what you want to do, when you want to do it, and how you want to do it.

Practice Forgiveness

You've been through a lot already, and it's difficult when life throws you lemons again. But hey, only you can forgive yourself, and you don't need anyone's validation. Life has its own ups and downs, and you could feel discouraged and out of control, but try as much as you can to practice forgiveness. Offer the fresh start that you need and, if necessary, meet a therapist who can help you recenter your new routine and life.

Reach Out to Friends

No matter what your circumstances, your social network is a great support system. If you're struggling to adjust to your new life, seek help from people who empathize with you. Leaning on close friends and family members is crucial during your transition. They could also have a few tips and comfort words to help you regain your self-confidence.

Remember Self-Care

It takes a lot of work to adapt to a routine, and that work can drain you. It's essential to take care of your physical and emotional well-being by regularly exercising, practicing a hobby, and spending time with loved ones and nature. The ideal self-care routine could differ from person to person, and hence, anything that reduces your stress, like cycling or reading a book, can also be included.

Be Present and Keep In Touch

Don't forget important meetings or days. It could be a friend's birthday or your parents wedding anniversary; try to be a part of every event. It could also be work meetings or volunteer meet-ups—anything that helps you keep your social circle active is important.

Get Rid of Negative Influences

As discussed in the previous chapter, it's important for you to steer clear of negative influences, especially if you're just out of prison, because there is a high chance you'll end up back in jail if you're under the influence of a bad company. Get rid of your old circles and find new friends or support groups. Understand who is toxic and who brings out the best in you; this is especially important because life after prison can be difficult, and you don't want to end up being helpless.

Reflect and Take Stock

Now that you're out of prison, you will find yourself with more time than you had as an inmate. Hence, it's time to plan ahead and think about your next steps. Look at yourself a couple of months or a year down the lane. What do you want to do?

Practice Gratitude

If you're out of prison today, a lot of people have likely helped. Do not forget the path you traversed and the people that guided you. It's important to practice gratitude and, if possible, give it back to society in every way possible.

Consider All Challenges

Sometimes, you could fall into a relapse or back into old habits. For example, if you plan on working early, your challenge could be in getting enough sleep the night before. You might find it hard to coordinate your schedules. However, do not let the presence of challenges worry you and deter you from establishing new habits.

Set Up a 30-Day Challenge

Studies show that habits which are performed daily become a part of your routine in 21 days. In most cases, you fail to cultivate good habits simply because you cannot stick to them. Fix a date and launch your action plan for 30 days straight; if you miss a day, then count all over again until you are consistent. Remember to not be hard on yourself.

Hold Yourself Publicly Accountable

The most valuable tool is your support network. Be it your best friend, partner, or anyone else online or offline, being accountable to someone other than you will help you stick to your goal. If a person has a group or team of supporters who follow them or look up to them, that person is more likely to stick to habits. If, for instance, you believe that you need to work on yourself to save your marriage, then keep yourself accountable to your spouse.

Overcome Setbacks

Life happens, and our willpower can run out. We could get swayed from our goals by life getting in the way. If something stops you or affects your schedule, one way to tackle the issue is to evaluate it and see how you can get through, around, or over the situation. However if you've established a routine, it becomes part of your life, and stress is less likely to interrupt you or throw you off your routine.

Talk to a Counselor

You don't have to adjust to your new routine on your own. There are mental health counseling services, which are a great resource for those undergoing a stressful transition. A professional can guide you with specific tools that will help you cope with this new life change. A counselor is also your safe space to talk about your challenges, victories, or even thoughts. You will soon find yourself coping better with the help of a counselor.

Mind Your Money

Beyond finding a job after prison, you must be aware of financial surprises that could show up every now and then. Look out for taxes, insurance, and other costs that can undo months of earnings. Check due dates to avoid penalties; make sure you pay all the monthly bills at the scheduled time. Develop a detailed budget and cut whatever takes too much of your money. Reevaluate your insurance coverage and cut all debts. Remember to have retirement savings as well.

Ways to Help Your Partner Adjust to An After-Prison Life

This section is for those who are expecting their partner's release day. It could be the most nervous yet overwhelming moment for a long time. While you prepare for their homecoming with excitement and anticipation, it's also essential to prepare yourself to help them adjust to their life post-incarceration.

There are many things you can do to help your loved one—

Listen to Them: Nothing is more precious than being the listener while you let another person speak. They could have plenty of stories to tell you; they might also be going through culture shock when they return. Sometimes, ex-prisoners also go through a lot of stress and feel anxious. If so, stop everything you're doing and pay attention; give them the space to talk and self-regulate.

Do Not Insist That They Do Things: It is so easy to insist your partner come along with you wherever you go or do everything you ask them to. However, remember that they've been incarcerated for so long that they've forgotten how to socialize; they could be feeling anxious about meeting your friends and family. So, give them the time they need to recover and be fully ready to step out. Let them decide what they need to do at their own pace. Giving them a choice to make a decision that will help them feel more in control of their life.

Be There: The best thing you can do for your partner is to be there for them as they learn to navigate in this new world. Stay by their side always, whether at the grocery store, restaurant table, family gatherings, church or school events, or any other setting that's unfamiliar or intimidating for them.

Don't Do Everything For Them: Be a teacher, not a helper. It may be easy to do everything for your partner, but for how long? You must prepare them to be on their own and learn to do things by themselves. Teach them how to do something that empowers them—for example, paying bills through online banking, operating electronics, and so on. When you do everything for them, you'll either get frustrated, or they'll start feeling incompetent.

Show Them Respect: Everyone experiences prison differently, and hence, they change too. They're not the same person you knew before prison. You must get to know this person and respect their opinions, especially when they're contrary to yours. Let them have their own voice and way of doing things. When they feel respected, they'll have the confidence to face any obstacle on their own and walk with assurance.

The time it takes for anyone to get adjusted to a new life depends on how long they've been locked up. Finding your footing after prison is an uphill battle. Still, don't give up when days are tough; remember you're figuring things out, and it takes time. Be kind to yourself.

Conclusion

Prison life can be hard, but just because you've been through it doesn't mean you get stuck in the vicious prison cycle, go in and out of prison your whole life, pass the blame, and choose to never change yourself. Times can be so overwhelming that you could feel it's impossible to change. No one has ever mastered their mental strength entirely, but with proper resources and tools provided in this book, you'll be able to smash through these challenges.

Key Takeaways From the Book:

- The first part of the book talks about changes that occur within prison.

    - Self-identity is important. Do not forget who you are and where you came from.

    - Stick to your goals and follow these strategies: visualize your success, start now instead of later, break your goals into smaller steps, and surround yourself with positivity.

    - Education is important, and it is a great step to achieve your goals outside prison. It helps you effectively re enter into the society and find a job. Education is also known to reduce violence and crime by 75%.

- Mental health is an important factor in prison life and after. It's important to talk to someone as a way to reduce the stress, anxiety, and depression associated with imprisonment.

- Addressing mental health issues will improve overall wellbeing and quality of life.

- Use your time in prison wisely by improving your health through exercise and proper diet. Eat the right foods and get active by means of stretching, aerobics, and resistance activities like push-ups and sit-ups.

- The second part of the book dives into changes outside prison and the importance of having support groups and a community.

  - With support groups, you will feel wanted and less lonely. This reduces stress, depression, and anxiety.

- Support is available through government departments and agencies, and at community centers, churches, and neighbourhood houses, as well as emergency relief agencies.

- Maintaining healthy relationships outside prison with friends and family will motivate you to adjust to your new life and keep you from recidivism.

- Giving back to society through volunteering programs will give you a sense of purpose and positivity.

- Being part of a social network will prevent you from committing crimes.

- Physical benefits of volunteering include stress reduction and reduced feelings of rage and animosity. Research shows that helping others might even help us live longer.

- Find the right influence you need to reenter society the right way. If your best friend is a great role model, consider them as a mentor. If you believe one of your family members can give you the mentorship that you need, seek their help.

- You can give back to society in several ways: donate your time, perform an act of kindness, be a part of charity events, help a child in need, volunteer at a senior centre, plant a tree, get into recycling, or become a mentor for ex-convicts.

- Get back into education after release. It's especially important if you're seeking a job opportunity.

- There are several education programs for ex-prisoners: Work Opportunity for Tax Credits (WOTC), The Federal Bonding Program, Fair Chance Pledge, and Fair Chance Employers.

- You need to get a driver's license, a permanent address, learn the transportation system, get a phone number, and consider counseling before you apply for schools.

- Stay clear from negative influences that contrast with your individual restraints, comfort levels, and what you believe is right and wrong. Encourage yourself to stick to these restraints in all scenarios.

- Understand your own individual needs and goals before entering group settings.

- You have probably made some tough choices because of negative influences that have landed you in prison in the first place. Don't go back to these old habits. Avoiding them is the first step to clearing negative influences. If you think you live in a neighborhood filled with criminals or crime, then it's time for a change.

- Beware of negative impacts on your mental health. Find therapy if nothing helps. When negative thoughts are in your mind, pushing you to fall back into your old habits, communication is the best way to get them out of your head.

- Nothing is more negative than rejection. Especially when you are applying to schools or jobs, rejection can hurt, and it can lead you to doing some regretful actions if you aren't able to control your anger. Remember to go easy on yourself.

- Encourage yourself to focus on your ultimate desired outcome rather than your past failures.

- Create a positive routine that you can stick to once you're out of jail.

- A daily routine will help you calm down when you're fresh out of prison. Your regimen doesn't need to be elaborate.

- A routine will help make sure you keep things on track, make sure your life has a purpose, and stick to the same frequency of activities. This is the final step in getting your life back together.

Remember not to fear challenges, because they make you greater. Each person you meet is your teacher, and you need to be the master of your own destiny. Be honest to yourself and others; unless you start doing something different to change your life, you are stuck at the same place. You don't need a lot to be happy in life; the fact that you're out of prison or will be soon should make you spread your wings and live life to the fullest. This is the moment to take action, change your life, and find the success you've always dreamed of. Don't give up—find your passion, find your base, and reenter society with your head held high.

So, what do you think? Did this book answer all your questions? Do you think it's worth a recommendation? If so, pass it on, and don't forget to let me know what you think.

References

5 Tips for Adjusting to New Routines. (2021, February 5). The Collective. https://www.collectivebh.com/post/5-tips-for-adjusting-to-new-routines

10 Helpful Ways For Giving Back to the Community. (2015, June 11). Lotsa Helping Hands. https://lotsahelpinghands.com/blog/giving-back-to-the-community/

A. (2021a, March 24). *15 Insanely Simple Ways To Say Goodbye To Negativity.* Amie Flanagan. http://www.amieflanagan.com/15-insanely-simple-ways-to-say-goodbye-to-negativity/

Acevedo, M. (2020, December 15). *Benefits of Higher Education for Formerly Incarcerated People.* Institute for Research on Labor and Employment. https://irle.berkeley.edu/benefits-of-higher-education-for-formerly-incarcerated-people/

After an Arrest | NAMI: National Alliance on Mental Illness. (n.d.). NAMI. Retrieved September 23, 2021, from https://www.nami.org/Your-Journey/Individuals-with-Mental-Illness/Reentry-After-a-Period-of-Incarceration

After-prison support | Corrections, Prisons and Parole. (n.d.). Corrections Prison & Parole. Retrieved September 17, 2021, from https://www.corrections.vic.gov.au/release/after-prison-support

Alleyne, C. (2018, November 13). *30 Ways to Give Back to Your Community.* Country Living. https://www.countryliving.com/life/g24995021/giving-back-community/?slide=1

Ancelmo, M. (2018, March 5). *Mentoring — Giving your share back to the community.* Medium. https://medium.com/@marceloancelmo/mentoring-giving-your-share-back-to-the-community-23abfc7adb22

Back to School Routine | Ways to Adjust to a New Routine for Kids. (n.d.). Tinies. Retrieved September 22, 2021, from https://www.tinies.com/our-favourites/ways-to-adjust-to-a-new-routine.html

Baker, K. (2020, May 29). *Top tips on how to adapt to your new routine.* Holistic. https://www.holisticgroup.co.uk/blog/top-tips-on-how-to-adapt-to-your-new-routine

Benefits after Incarceration. (n.d.). Ssa Gov. Retrieved September 23, 2021, from https://www.ssa.gov/reentry/benefits.htm

Benefits of Community Service – Community Engagement. (n.d.). Western Connecticut State University. Retrieved September 21, 2021, from https://www.wcsu.edu/community-engagement/benefits-of-volunteering/

Blocked for legal reasons. (2019, August 5). Sfgate. https://blog.sfgate.com/lifestyle/2019/08/05/back-on-your-feet-7-tips-for-adjusting-to-life-after-incarceration/

Brown, T. (2020, August 28). *17 Ways To Give Back To The Community In A Meaningful Way* MobileAxept. https://mobileaxept.com/2020/06/19/ways-to-give-back-to-the-community/

A Call for Effective Emergency Management in Correctional Facilities During COVID-19. (2020, July 31). Center for American Progress. https://www.americanprogress.org/issues/criminal-justice/news/2020/07/31/488408/call-effective-emergency-management-correctional-facilities-covid-19/

Canada, B. P. W. (2019, June 9). *Maintaining A Relationship From Prison - Beyond Prison Walls Canada.* Medium. https://medium.com/@BeyondPrisonWallsCnda/maintaining-a-relationship-from-prison-79870e848d73

Center for Employment Opportunities. (2021, July 9). CEO. https://ceoworks.org/

Chen, G. (2021, August 14). *Sending Prisoners Back to School? A New IHEP Study Says Yes.* Community College Review. https://www.communitycollegereview.com/blog/sending-prisoners-back-to-school-a-new-ihep-study-says-yes

Child Support and Incarceration. (n.d.). NCSL. Retrieved September 23, 2021, from https://www.ncsl.org/research/human-services/child-support-and-incarceration.aspx

Children of Incarcerated Parents. (n.d.). Youth Government. Retrieved September 23, 2021, from https://youth.gov/youth-topics/children-of-incarcerated-parents

Cohen, J. (2013, September 11). *Do You Want To Change Your Life For The Better? 7 Ways To Make It A Habit.* Forbes.

https://www.forbes.com/sites/jennifercohen/2013/09/11/do-you-want-to-change-your-life-for-the-better-7-ways-to-make-it-a-habit/?sh=1b1e4b86398e

Continue with education - Prisoners & #039; Education Trust. (2021, February 16). Prisoners' Education Trust. https://www.prisonerseducation.org.uk/get-support/people-leaving-prison/continue-with-education/

Corona, V. (2021, June 11). *7 Tips to Have a Healthy Relationship with an Inmate.* Scholarlyoa.Com. https://scholarlyoa.com/healthy-relationship-with-inmate/

Department for Correctional Services - Community Mentor Program. (n.d.). Government of South Australia. Retrieved September 23, 2021, from https://www.corrections.sa.gov.au/volunteers/volunteer-programs/community-mentor-program

Department for Correctional Services - Other support groups. (n.d.). Government of South Australia. Retrieved September 23, 2021, from https://www.corrections.sa.gov.au/volunteers/other-support-groups

Disaster Financial Assistance. (n.d.). USA Gov. Retrieved September 23, 2021, from https://www.usa.gov/disaster-financial-help

Domestic Violence Facts, Types & Effects. (2019, January 14). MedicineNet. https://www.medicinenet.com/domestic_violence/article.htm

Drop, G. (2021, June 25). *Ways To Give Back To Your Community on a Budget*. Green Drop. https://www.gogreendrop.com/blog/ways-to-give-back-to-your-community-on-a-budget/

Education Opportunities in Prison Are Key to Reducing Crime. (2018, November 30). Center for American Progress. https://www.americanprogress.org/issues/education-k-12/news/2018/03/02/447321/education-opportunities-prison-key-reducing-crime/

Ex-Offender Mentoring: Training Volunteers to Serve as Mentors in MN. (n.d.). Volunteers of America: National. Retrieved September 23, 2021, from https://www.voa.org/videos/ex-offender-mentoring-training-volunteers-to-serve-as-mentors-in-mn

G. (n.d.-a). *4 Ways to Give Back to Your Community*. Gaiam. Retrieved September 21, 2021, from https://www.gaiam.com/blogs/discover/4-ways-to-give-back-to-your-community

G. (2020a, October 6). *Tips for Establishing Your Post-Coronavirus Routine*. Cleveland Clinic. https://health.clevelandclinic.org/tips-for-establishing-your-post-coronavirus-routine/

Gani, F. (2019, May 7). *How to Find a Mentor and Maintain a Meaningful Relationship*. Zapier. https://zapier.com/blog/how-to-find-a-mentor/

Giving Back Through Mentoring. (n.d.). PharmaVOICE. Retrieved September 21, 2021, from https://www.pharmavoice.com/article/giving-back-through-mentoring/

H. (2019, October 28). *Healthy Relationships Have Boundaries, Not Prison Bars*. Thought Catalog. https://thoughtcatalog.com/holly-riordan/2019/07/healthy-relationships-have-boundaries-not-prison-bars/

Homelessness and Prisoner Re-Entry: Examining Barriers to Housing. (n.d.). Volunteers of America: National. Retrieved September 18, 2021, from https://www.voa.org/homelessness-and-prisoner-reentry

House, T. G. (2019, October 24). *How Do People in Recovery Let Go of Bad Influences in Their Lives?* The Guest House. https://www.theguesthouseocala.com/how-do-people-in-recovery-let-go-of-bad-influences-in-their-lives/

How to Integrate Back Into Society After Serving Time. (2020, February 17). Jared Justice. https://www.jaredjustice.com/blog/how-to-integrate-back-into-society-after-serving-time/

How to look after your mental health in prison. (2019, March 8). Mental Health Foundation. https://www.mentalhealth.org.uk/publications/how-look-after-your-mental-health-prison

Huerta, M. (2019, April 10). *Parenting From Prison: It's Not Impossible.* Kars4Kids Parenting. https://parenting.kars4kids.org/parenting-prison/

I. (2021b, September 11). *Cutting Negative Influences from Your Life.* Renaissance Recovery. https://www.renaissancerecovery.com/cutting-negative-influences-from-your-life/

The Implementation of Inmate Mentor Programs in the Correctional Treatment System as an Innovative Approach. (n.d.). Taylor & Francis. Retrieved September 23, 2021, from https://www.tandfonline.com/doi/abs/10.1080/15332700802418758?journalCode=wtad20

Indeed Editorial Team. (2021, July 26). *How Do I Create and Stick To a Daily Schedule?* Indeed Career Guide. https://www.indeed.com/career-advice/career-development/create-a-daily-schedule

Initiative, P. P. (n.d.-a). *Criminal justice responses to the coronavirus pandemic.* Prison Policy Initiative. Retrieved September 23, 2021, from https://www.prisonpolicy.org/virus/virusresponse.html

Initiative, P. P. (n.d.-b). *Getting Back on Course: Educational exclusion and attainment among formerly incarcerated people.* Prison Policy Initiative. Retrieved September 22, 2021, from https://www.prisonpolicy.org/reports/education.html

Initiative, P. P. (n.d.-c). *Legal resources.* Prison Policy Initiative. Retrieved September 18, 2021, from https://www.prisonpolicy.org/resources/legal/

Initiative, P. P. (n.d.-d). *Mental Health*. Prison Policy Initiative. Retrieved September 23, 2021, from https://www.prisonpolicy.org/research/mental_health/

Initiative, P. P. (n.d.-e). *Out of Prison & Out of Work*. Prison Policy Initiative. Retrieved September 19, 2021, from https://www.prisonpolicy.org/reports/outofwork.html

Jannasch, N. (2015, October 23). *How To Say Goodbye To A Friend Who Is A Bad Influence –*. TeenLife. https://www.teenlife.com/blog/how-say-goodbye-friend-who-bad-influence/

Jarrett, C. (n.d.). *How prison changes people*. BBC Future. Retrieved September 22, 2021, from https://www.bbc.com/future/article/20180430-the-unexpected-ways-prison-time-changes-people

Job Seekers Who Were Formerly Incarcerated. (n.d.). Careers Centre. Retrieved September 19, 2021, from https://careers.usc.edu/students/diversity-resources/formerly-incarcerated/

Jocelyn Fontaine, Jennifer Biess. (2021, April). *Housing as a Platform for Formerly Incarcerated Persons*. Urban Institute.

https://www.urban.org/sites/default/files/publication/25321/412552-Housing-as-a-Platform-for-Formerly-Incarcerated-Persons.PDF

Last Prisoner Project Covid19 Emergency Relief Fund. (n.d.). Last Prisoner Project. Retrieved September 23, 2021, from https://give.lastprisonerproject.org/campaign/last-prisoner-project-covid19-emergency-relief-fund/c278584

Lawyers and Legal Advice. (n.d.). USA Gov. Retrieved September 18, 2021, from https://www.usa.gov/legal-aid

Legal Services, Prisoners' Attitudes and "Rehabilitation" on JSTOR. (n.d.). JSTOR. Retrieved September 18, 2021, from https://www.jstor.org/stable/1142569

Leonard, J. (2020, August 7). *What are the effects of solitary confinement on health?* Medical News Today. https://www.medicalnewstoday.com/articles/solitary-confinement-effects#reasons-for-use

Lindsay. (2021, March 25). *5 ways you can give back to your community (even under lockdown) | Less waste, less stuff, sustainable living.* Treading My Own Path. https://treadingmyownpath.com/2021/03/25/ways-you-can-give-back/

Llopis, G. (2015, March 30). *5 Ways To Find Mentors And Make Them Matter.* Forbes. https://www.forbes.com/sites/glennllopis/2012/03/26/5-ways-to-find-mentors-and-make-it-matter/?sh=3be0d96f58d0

M. (2020b, November 30). *A Guide To Finding Housing After Incarceration.* MYMOVE. https://www.mymove.com/moving/guides/moving-after-incarceration/

M. (2021c, July 7). *How to Overcome Negative Influences on Behavior.* Sanjeev Datta Personality School. https://sanjeevdatta.com/how-to-overcome-negative-influences/

Mentoring 101: Why giving back is important to keep skills and careers vibrant. (2018, May 31). Adobe Blog. https://blog.adobe.com/en/publish/2018/05/31/mentoring-101-giving-back-important-keep-skills-careers-vibrant.html#gs.baggage

Monster. (n.d.). *These tips can help you adjust to the changes a new job and new schedule entail.* Monster Career Advice. Retrieved September 22, 2021, from https://www.monster.com/career-advice/article/new-job-work-schedule

Nature Editorial. (n.d.). *Moving from prison to a PhD.* Nature. Retrieved September 22, 2021, from https://www.nature.com/articles/d41586-019-03370-1?error=cookies_not_supported&code=e5a861 68-21e5-4464-8667-dca0f19b6d07

The online support groups for former inmates and their loved ones. (2018, June 10). The Outline. https://theoutline.com/post/4904/the-online-support-groups-for-former-inmates-and-their-loved-ones

P., P., & P. (n.d.-b). *Prioritizing, Parenting, and Protecting Our Children.* Parenting Inside Out. Retrieved September 23, 2021, from http://www.parentinginsideout.org/

A Pledge to Give Back. (2017, September 27). Beyond Prison. https://www.beyondprison.us/chapter/a-pledge-to-give-back/

Post Incarceration and Housing Services - John Howard Society of Toronto. (2021, May 12). John Howard Society of Ontario. https://johnhoward.on.ca/toronto/services/post-incarceration-housing-services/

Prison Fellowship. (2018, March 6). *How to Find a Job After Prison - Job Search.* https://www.prisonfellowship.org/resources/s

upport-friends-family-of-prisoners/supporting-successful-prisoner-reentry/how-to-find-a-job-after-prison/

Prison Parenting Programs: Resources for Parenting Instructors in. (2021, January 14). National Institute of Corrections. https://nicic.gov/prison-parenting-programs-resources-parenting-instructors-prisons-and-jails

prison parenting programs: Topics by WorldWideScience.org. (n.d.). World Wide Science. Retrieved September 23, 2021, from https://worldwidescience.org/topicpages/p/prison+parenting+programs.html

Prison Policy Initiative. (2013, January). *Legal Services for People in Prison and Jail*. Prison Legal News. https://www.prisonlegalnews.org/media/publications/pln_list_of_legal_services_jails_and_prisons_jan_2013.pdf

Prisoner mentor program aims to reduce recidivism rates. (2018, March 3). AP NEWS. https://apnews.com/article/e299f76a31a3497eb9ff085694ce7723

Prisoners & #39; Rights. (n.d.). Pro Bono. Retrieved September 18, 2021, from https://www.probono.net/prisoners/

Project 39A — Legal Aid. (n.d.). Project 39A. Retrieved September 18, 2021, from https://www.project39a.com/legal-aid

Protecting the constitutional rights of people behind bars through advocacy, education and litigation. (2021, July 17). Prison Law Office. https://prisonlaw.com/

Provide Post Release Employment Services. (n.d.). NIC. Retrieved September 19, 2021, from https://info.nicic.gov/cirs/node/40

Re-entry after prison groups. (n.d.). Meetup. Retrieved September 23, 2021, from https://www.meetup.com/topics/re-entry-after-prison/

Reentry and Employment for the Formerly Incarcerated and the Role of American Trades Unions. (2016, April 6). National Employment Law Project. https://www.nelp.org/publication/reentry-and-employment-for-the-formerly-incarcerated-and-the-role-of-american-trades-unions/

Research Guides: Reentry and Employment Resources for Justice-Involved Individuals: Employment Resources. (n.d.). Library of Congress. Retrieved September 19, 2021, from https://guides.loc.gov/reentry-resources/employment

Resources, S. I. H. (2021, August 20). *5 Ways to Give Back to Your Community*. Society Insurance. https://societyinsurance.com/blog/5-ways-to-give-back-to-your-community/

Returning to Work After Prison. (2017, April 24). MDRC. https://www.mdrc.org/publication/returning-work-after-prison

Robinson, L. (2021, April 19). *Volunteering and its Surprising Benefits*. HelpGuide.Org. https://www.helpguide.org/articles/healthy-living/volunteering-and-its-surprising-benefits.htm

Rominger, A. (2021, April 7). *Why Volunteer? 7 Benefits of Volunteering that Will Inspire You to Take Action*. Grow Ensemble. https://growensemble.com/why-volunteer/

Safety Plan. (n.d.). Safety Plan. Retrieved September 23, 2021, from https://www.mctxsheriff.org/residents/victim_services/safety_plans.php

Safety Plan for the Victim. (n.d.). Safe and Fear-Free Environment. Retrieved September 23, 2021, from http://www.safebristolbay.org/safety-planning.html

Safety Planning. (n.d.). Crime Victims Assistance Center, Inc. Retrieved September 23, 2021, from http://www.cvac.us/safety-planning.html

Safety Tips. (2019, November 26). WomensLaw.Org. https://www.womenslaw.org/about-abuse/safety-tips

Safety When an Abuser Gets Out of Jail. (2021, August 5). WomensLaw.Org. https://www.womenslaw.org/about-abuse/safety-tips/safety-when-abuser-gets-out-jail

Hope where it's needed most. (n.d.). Salvation Army. Retrieved September 17, 2021, from https://www.salvationarmy.org.au/

Say Goodbye to Negative Thoughts. (n.d.). Break Through. Retrieved September 22, 2021, from http://www.breakthroughpsychologyprogram.com/say-goodbye-to-negative-thoughts.html

Shelburne, B. (2019, April 14). *Out of prison and giving back*. Https://Www.Wtvm.Com. https://www.wtvm.com/2019/04/13/out-prison-giving-back/

St Vincent de Paul Society Australia. (2021, September 9). *Poverty in Australia is of great concern to us.* https://www.vinnies.org.au/

Staff, T. (2021, September 3). *Prison Education: Guide to College Degrees for Inmates and Ex-Offenders.* TheBestSchools.Org. https://thebestschools.org/magazine/prison-inmate-education-guide/

Supported housing for prisoners returning to the community | Corrections, Prisons and Parole. (n.d.). Corrections, Prisons and Parole. Retrieved September 18, 2021, from https://www.corrections.vic.gov.au/supported-housing-for-prisoners-returning-to-the-community

Supporting Children and Families Affected by Parental Incarceration - Child Welfare Information Gateway. (n.d.). Child Welfare. Retrieved September 23, 2021, from https://www.childwelfare.gov/topics/supporting/support-services/incarceration/

Tesema, M. (n.d.). *Creating A New Routine Matters Now More Than Ever.* Shine. Retrieved September 22, 2021, from

https://advice.theshineapp.com/articles/creating-a-new-routine-matters-now-more-than-ever/

the Annie E. Casey Foundation, Public/Private Ventures. (2021, May 26). *Mentoring Formerly Incarcerated Adults*. The Annie E. Casey Foundation. https://www.aecf.org/resources/mentoring-formerly-incarcerated-adults

Tijerina, C. (2021, January 13). *5 Ways to Help Your Loved One Adjust to Life After Prison*. TYRO Blog. https://tyro.blog/family/5-ways-to-help-your-loved-one-adjust-to-life-after-prison/

Tips to Support Children When a Parent is in Prison. (n.d.). HealthyChildren.Org. Retrieved September 23, 2021, from https://www.healthychildren.org/English/healthy-living/emotional-wellness/Building-Resilience/Pages/Tips-to-Support-Children-When-a-Parent-is-in-Prison.aspx

Today, C. (2020, March 16). *Counseling in jail*. Counseling Today. https://ct.counseling.org/2020/03/counseling-in-jail/#

Together We Rise. (2020, August 20). *7 Ways to Give Back to the Community*.

https://www.togetherwerise.org/blog/7-ways-give-back-community/

TReND Wyoming. (2020, April 23). *5 Tips to Help a Family Member Reintegrate After Prison Release*. https://www.trendwyoming.org/articles/helping-family-member-reintegrate-after-prison-release/

U.S. Probation Officer, District of New Jersey. (2013, June). *Overcoming Legal Barriers to Reentry*. Syracuse University College of Law. https://www.uscourts.gov/sites/default/files/77_1_1_0.pdf

Vertava Health. (2020, December 30). *Dual Diagnosis: Post Incarceration Syndrome and Therapy after Prison*. https://vertavahealth.com/dual-diagnosis/post-incarceration-syndrome/

Visher, C. (2008, October). *Employment after Prison: A Longitudinal Study of Releasees in Three States*. Urban Institute Justice Policy Center. https://www.urban.org/sites/default/files/publication/32106/411778-Employment-after-Prison-A-Longitudinal-Study-of-Releasees-in-Three-States.PDF

Watkin, J. (2015, April 29). *5 Reasons To Say Goodbye To Negativity*. Customer Service Life.

https://customerservicelife.com/5-reasons-to-say-goodbye-to-negativity/

Webster, R. (2021, June 21). *Helping offenders & #039; families.* Russell Webster. https://www.russellwebster.com/resource-packs/helping-offenders-families/

What happens if a parent that should pay child support is in jail? - MassLegalHelp. (n.d.). MassLegalHelp. Retrieved September 23, 2021, from https://www.masslegalhelp.org/children-and-families/child-support/in-jail

Where âReturning Citizensâ Find Housing After Prison. (2019, April 23). The Pew Charitable Trusts. https://www.pewtrusts.org/en/research-and-analysis/blogs/stateline/2019/04/23/where-returning-citizens-find-housing-after-prison

Writers, S. (2020, August 14). *Career & College Guide for Formerly Incarcerated People.* Public Service Degrees. https://www.publicservicedegrees.org/resources/education-and-careers-after-incarceration/

Made in the USA
Las Vegas, NV
30 June 2023